HOW TO MARKET TO PEOPLE NOT LIKE YOU

HOW TO MARKET TO PEOPLE NOT LIKE YOU

"KNOW IT OR BLOW IT" RULES FOR REACHING DIVERSE CUSTOMERS

KELLY McDONALD

WILEY
John Wiley & Sons, Inc.

Published by John Wiley & Sons, Inc., Hoboken, New Jersey.
Published simultaneously in Canada.

For general information on our other products and services or for technical support, please contact our Customer Care Department within the United States at (800) 762-2974, outside the United States at (317) 572-3993 or fax (317) 572-4002.

Wiley also publishes its books in a variety of electronic formats. Some content that appears in print may not be available in electronic books. For more information about Wiley products, visit our web site at www.wiley.com.

Library of Congress Cataloging-in-Publication Data:

McDonald, Kelly, 1961-
    How to market to people not like you : "know it or blow it" rules for reaching diverse customers / Kelly McDonald.
        p. cm.
Includes index.
    ISBN 978-0-470-87900-9 (hardback); ISBN 978-1-118-01498-1 (ebk);
ISBN 978-1-118-01499-8 (ebk); ISBN 978-1-118-01500-1 (ebk)
    1. Marketing. 2. Consumer satisfaction. I. Title.
    HF5415.M3795 2011
    658.8–dc22   2010039794

Printed in the United States of America

10 9 8 7 6 5 4 3

To Jennifer Martin, for being a better
friend than I thought was possible.
To John, para siempre.
And to Nancy, for taking a chance on me in the first place.

Contents

Acknowledgments

There are so many people who helped me with this book—whether it was with their wisdom, their insights, their support, or their patience. "Thank you" doesn't really express the depth of my gratitude, but I don't have any other words.

To my editor, Richard Narramore, for his steady, supportive coaching and patience with my endless questions. And for his phone call, which got the whole ball rolling to begin with.

To my "readers," those who read and re-read draft after draft and offered their critiques and comments: Melinda Fishman, Jennifer Martin, Dennis DuPont, Melissa Timmerman, Iris Goldfeder, Stuart Gaffney, Karen Eaton, Daniel Eaton, Kim Edwards, Trace Symonds, Traci Thrasher, and John Barry.

To the panelists: Frances Gannon, Nina Kersten, Aimee Valentine, Kim Edwards, Tajana Mesic, Domineice Reese, Kimberly Brandon, Priscilla Anthony, Tiffanie Chiles-Mitchell, Carissa Mavec, Melissa Lewis, Shannelle Mosley, Percy Bryant III, Robert Swafford, Tim

Bennett, Todd Young, Joel Benjamin Griffin, Karen Eaton, Melissa Timmerman, Garrett Griffin, and Frank Fardatta.

To Liliana Ramírez, for keeping the company running smoothly and taking care of business while I wrote the book. You did, and do, a fantastic job, always.

To those who contributed with answers, insights, and suggestions: Tim Bennett, Stuart Gaffney, José Puente, Jay Baer, and Juli Black.

To those who listened to me rant or whine when I felt stressed—probably everyone I know, but especially John, Melinda, Jennifer, Melissa, and Liliana. Your daily calls, emails, texts, and hugs kept me sane.

And to my clients, for their support, patience, and enthusiasm while the book was being written.

Introduction

You Can't Reach a Customer You Don't Understand

I was in the Dallas airport recently and saw one of the worst ads I've ever seen. It stopped me in my tracks and I found myself studying it, trying to fathom how an ad this awful came to exist. As a marketing professional, I had to wonder, "Who created it? And who approved it?" The ad was for Cancun, Mexico. The intent was obviously to increase tourism to Cancun by appealing to vacationers. It was an ad featuring a beautiful beach with a woman lying on a massage table, outside, by the ocean, getting a massage. There were starfish and sand dollars strewn around the bottom of the ad. The headline stated: "Yes You Can . . . Cun."

Aside from the cheesy, stupid, horrible play on words and pun ("Yes you can"), there was nothing that would entice a reader to choose Cancun over any other beach destination. There was no mention of the culture, the history, or things to do in Cancun. There was simply a picture of a woman getting a massage by the ocean. It could have been an ad for Miami or St. Croix or San Diego. The odd thing is, there are many, many reasons why someone would want to vacation in Cancun: world-class snorkeling and diving, Mayan ruins, five-star hotels and restaurants, fantastic weather, a large English-speaking population, affordability—the list goes on. I'm willing to bet that most people planning a vacation to a beach destination are not going to choose their destination because of a generic, bland ad and a corny, cheesy pun with no relevance.

It was kind of sad, too. Poor Cancun—if Cancun were a person, he'd feel so misunderstood! Imagine the thoughts Cancun would have: "Wow, I have so much to offer! I have rich cultural history; amazing ruins and temples that are thousands of years old; a terrific, mild climate; clear turquoise waters filled with fish and colorful coral; great restaurants and nightlife; and I'm so affordable compared to others! So why is all of this substance overlooked in favor of making a cheesy pun? Doesn't anybody know who I am? Don't the ad makers want to know more about me and really understand me? If they did, and they created an ad that really showcased who I am, their results would be so much better! Because the people who really want what I have would learn about me. And they'd like what they learned. They'd want to come visit me and see for themselves. They'd want to experience me, the real Cancun."

To me, the reason that ad for Cancun was so weak was that whoever created it doesn't seem to know anything about what vacationers want. It didn't communicate effectively—about the merits of Cancun or, frankly, anything. There was no substance to that message at all.

To be fair, it's hard to communicate effectively when you don't really understand whom you're talking to or what that person or group cares about. The best marketing messages resonate with their target audience; there is something in the message that taps into a belief, a value, an aspiration, a hope, a fear, or something the target holds dear. This is a simple concept, but it's scary because you don't want to risk offending anyone or making a fool of yourself if you try something new and get it wrong.

You're probably feeling some of that anxiety right now. The fact that you're even holding this book tells me that you know you need to reach out to new markets, you know there is a business opportunity in doing so, but how in the world do you begin? You want to grow your business, but you don't want to make a mistake or offend anyone. You know that a marketing message has to be relevant to the target audience, but how do you know what's "relevant" when the target audience is quite different from you or your experiences? How are you supposed to grasp someone's beliefs and values if that person is nothing like you?

That's what this book will address. It will teach you, step by step, how to market to people not like you. This is more important than ever because marketing budgets are getting tighter and tighter and the consumer market is more fragmented than ever. It's imperative that your marketing dollars work as well and as hard as they can to deliver potential prospects and customers to your business. This book will teach you what you need to know to reach new market segments without blowing it by making cultural blunders, foolish mistakes, or embarrassing errors. You can do it. And this book will show you how.

I have not met one person in the past several years who claims that growing business is easy. In fact, every business owner, corporate marketing manager, and ad agency or marketing executive tells me that their biggest business pressure, the thing that keeps them awake at night, is figuring out how to expand their business. There are really only three ways to do this:

1. Sell more of your products or services to your existing customer base, thereby increasing your sales volume or transaction revenue.
2. Get your customers to buy from you more frequently.
3. Tap into new market segments.

The first two options aren't all that realistic for many companies and brands. Let's say you're a car dealer. You might be able to sell your current customers a little more service (oil changes or accessories) with coupons and promotional efforts. Or you might be able to convince a customer to buy a new vehicle every three years instead of four. But each of these scenarios will bring only slight incremental revenue. If you want to really grow your business by selling more vehicles, you have to find new customers. The same is true if you're a restaurant owner; you can either try to get your current customers to come and dine more frequently, or you can try to sell them more food when they dine (appetizers, drinks, and desserts). But the better approach is to try to reach new customers who haven't eaten at your restaurant before.

By tapping into new markets and cultivating new customers, you gain sales immediately. Your sales growth won't be dependent on trying to change the behavior of your existing customers, which is very hard to do. You'll still have your existing customers, but you'll also have new customers, and those new customers represent huge potential for ongoing sales and profits.

It sounds simple, and it's quite logical: market to a new clientele and watch your business soar. Yet marketing to people who are not like you may make you feel very uncomfortable because there are so many examples of bad ads and horrible blunders out there. I know you may be afraid to even try to tap into a new market for fear of getting it wrong and making one of those embarrassing blunders. I promise that this book will show you the steps on how to do it right, without offending others or making a fool of yourself. Let me give you an example.

A couple of years ago, we were approached by an auto insurance company that specializes in nonstandard insurance, which means insurance for those with blemishes on their driving records or other problems. These individuals may have a poor driving record, a DUI offense, bad credit, no driver's license, and the like. You get the picture. They are individuals that other insurance companies do not want to insure because they're considered high risk.

This company, A-Affordable Insurance, wanted to reach out to Hispanic consumers in the Texas market. The first thing we did was conduct consumer focus groups among Hispanic adult drivers to learn what they thought about auto insurance. We discovered two primary things:

1. Everyone called it "car insurance," even if they had a truck or a sport-utility vehicle. They'd say, "Yes, I have car insurance on my truck" or "I pay $79 a month for the car insurance on my truck."

They didn't call it auto insurance—they called it car insurance, regardless of what type of vehicle they drove.

2. They didn't understand how insurance works. They found it all very confusing, particularly things like the deductible. One man stated in the focus groups that he felt he'd been ripped off by his insurance company. When we asked why, he said, "Because I'd been paying $120 a month for insurance for three years. When I finally had an accident, they told me I'd need to pay $500 to cover the deductible. What's that? Why don't they just take the money out of my account?" You can see how, if you are not very sophisticated about how insurance works, you might think that the money you've been paying for insurance goes into "an account" each month. And that the "account" will cover the repair expenses. Except that's not how it works, of course. We realized, hearing comments like these, that we really needed to do some education with this consumer before we could effectively sell him insurance.

The second thing we did was look at the other advertisers in that industry, to see and understand what the "competitive landscape" was like. We looked at TV spots, ads, and flyers to learn how the competition was positioning themselves and promoting themselves to the Hispanic nonstandard insurance consumer. What we found was quite interesting. All the companies going after this consumer were running very negative ads. The ads had messages like, "No credit? Bad credit? No money? Bad driving record? XYZ Insurance Company can help. . . ."

It struck us that, if you are the nonstandard insurance consumer, you already know you have poor credit. You already know you don't have much money. You already know you've got a bad driving record. You already have had to face up to these things and that probably doesn't make you feel very good about yourself. You don't need any reminders of the trouble you've had in the past or that you're currently facing. You need a solution, not a lecture about what a high-risk driver you are.

So we created a tagline for the client that took the opposite approach. We stated, in positive terms, that your business is welcome at A-Affordable insurance. The tagline in English said, "Car insurance for all." In Spanish, it was "Seguro de carros para todos."

To address the lack of understanding about insurance, we developed an educational seminar. We designed it to be 30 minutes long, explaining in clear, easy-to-understand terms how auto insurance works and why having auto insurance is important. We created inexpensive booklets that had all the basic information, in Spanish and English, about insurance. We included a glossary of terms, as well as a map of all the local A-Affordable offices with addresses and phone numbers.

We contacted local community centers, YMCAs, churches, and even laundromats and asked if we could present a free, no obligation, no sales pressure seminar on auto insurance. Because having auto insurance in Texas is required by law, everyone we approached said yes and provided the space for us to have the seminar at no cost to us. They considered it a positive message for the community. We posted flyers on-site about when the free seminar would be held.

We had bilingual agents from A-Affordable conduct the seminars. There was no hard sell—just an informative approach about auto insurance and what you need to know to protect yourself, your vehicle, and your loved ones. Of course, the agents provided their business cards to attendees, but it was positioned as, "If you have any questions, call me and let's talk." The agents were happy to do the seminars because they work on commission, and this opened up an entirely new customer group for them.

How did it work? Sales went up 19 percent during the campaign and calls to the company's dedicated Spanish-language 800 number increased 22 percent. What we did was quite simple: We talked to our target customer. We found out a few important things that helped us create a message that was relevant to them. We provided a solution for them (education about a topic they didn't fully understand). And we "put the welcome mat out" for them by creating a tagline that was positive and made them feel good about themselves instead of making them feel bad.

You can grow your business with sales results like this, by narrowcasting and following the steps to market to people not like you.

It's not that hard to do. And it's really important. Because the world is more diverse than ever, and not just racially and ethnically. Different viewpoints, lifestyles, levels of affluence, religions, values, and priorities are all ways in which we can be different from each other. No longer is there one "customer group," or what marketing folks like to call the "General Market." Technology has made it easier (and cheaper) than ever before for us to be recognized as individuals and have our needs and wants catered to by companies. For consumers, this has meant more information and, consequently, more choices. When you have more choices, you become more selective. The consumer today is more selective than ever before and has more power. Therefore, the marketer has to do a better job of reaching the consumer and making sure that the marketing message is not just received, but is received enthusiastically.

It all comes down to relevance. Sure, you can reach lots of people with your ads and marketing campaigns. But if you don't reach those people with a meaningful message that they find relevant to them, they'll dismiss you. That's what happened with the ad for Cancun; the ad reached me (I saw it and I read it), and then I immediately dismissed it. Because it had no real message and therefore, no real value to me. It was not relevant in any way.

It used to be easier. Back in the day, there just weren't that many ways to reach people, and consumers weren't as sophisticated as they are now. Mass marketing was easy. And we didn't have the ability to tailor our marketing messages and offers to specific, different audiences. Think about Nike. Decades ago, Nike launched their famous "Just Do It" campaign, and it was targeted to athletes and people who exercised. From there, Nike refined their marketing efforts because they realized that not all people who exercise are alike. They segmented their marketing messages and made them more targeted. Today, Nike markets to teens, women, various racial and ethnic groups, runners, basketball players, and those who participate in specialized sports. They even use the term *cross-training* to market to people who exercise in multiple ways, whether it's jumping rope, walking, or playing volleyball. Each message is different, and so are the media channels used to reach those different audiences.

You know that you need to cultivate new customers to ensure that your company thrives and grows. What you're probably struggling with is how to go about doing that. How do you find the right new market segment for your business? How do you develop meaningful, relevant messages? How do you know what a new customer group wants? How do you market in a new way to a new group and know that you're not offending, being culturally insensitive, or coming across as weird or stupid? Add to that the tremendous budget pressure that most businesses are under, and it's easy to see why you might be fearful about trying new techniques and approaches. You don't know how to market to people not like you. But you will.

In the following pages, you'll learn about market segments that represent high potential for your business. You'll recognize which are the best market segments for your business today and which represent opportunity in the future. You'll see that you don't need a huge budget to create meaningful marketing messages that will make the cash register ring.

You'll learn how to identify new market segments and reach them with relevance. You'll learn how to build a marketing message that will resonate with new customers without blowing it, offending, or being stereotypical or insensitive. You'll learn, step by step, what to do and what not to do.

Our world offers us a wealth of diversity. And this diversity will only expand in the future. Different cultures, languages, generations, and lifestyles bring huge, unlimited opportunity for growing your business. Diversity will drive everything from product development to consumer insights to marketing messages. It will shape culture, music, media, politics, entertainment, and religion. It will shape lifestyles and habits. It will present smart businesses with a wide-open playing field and a serious competitive edge.

Tap into this diverse marketplace and find your high-potential customer now. Learn how to market to people not like you and watch your business grow and prosper. You can do it.

PART ONE

Seven Steps for Selling to New and Unfamiliar Customers

CHAPTER ONE ▶

Get Out of Your Comfort Zone to Grow Sales

"SPRAY AND PRAY" VERSUS BROAD THINKING AND NARROWCASTING

Marketers are lazy. I should know—I'm a marketer. I don't mean to imply we don't work hard. We do. We work our butts off. And we tend to be unappreciated. There's even a joke about it in my field: "When business is great, the credit goes to the Sales Department. When business is bad, blame Marketing."

Marketing is hard. It's not like other disciplines in business that are easily measured or quantified. For example, if you're in the Product Development Department of a technology company and you develop a new computer system, you can test and test and retest that system to see where the bugs and glitches are before you ever release it for launch. In marketing, we can take certain steps to "test" our thinking, our approach, and our message, but it's still very hard to anticipate human behavior, desires, and what will ultimately inspire someone to buy something.

Marketers are also highly accountable for the results of their work. If you're a marketing executive at a company and your efforts don't yield the anticipated sales results, your butt's on the line. If you work for an ad agency and your clients don't get the results they want or expect, your clients will probably fire you. If you're a small business owner, your budget pressure is enormous and you need to make every dollar count.

When I say "marketers are lazy," what I mean by that is that we are often guilty of being lazy *thinkers*. We are under so much pressure to hit our numbers (sales targets or budget targets, or both), that we often take the path of least resistance or the easiest route to getting our work done. For example, sometimes marketing executives compromise on doing the *right* thing and end up doing the *safe* thing—the thing that makes their boss or their shareholders happy. Instead of marketing to your potential prospect, you end up marketing to yourself (or your boss).

I recently saw a brochure for a midsized accounting firm. Their potential customers are other businesses that need the services of a solid accounting firm. As a small business owner myself, I can say that some of the things that might be important to other business owners could be personal service, reasonable fees, excellent tax advice, financial problem solving, tax savings strategies, and long-range thinking and planning steps, just to name a few.

However, this brochure touted none of those attributes. Instead, it featured a picture of their building, and inside, a bio of their founder. It's hard to believe that anyone would choose an accounting firm based on what their building looks like. And most people are smart enough to know that the founder, if he or she is still alive, will not be the person actually working with you on your business.

The brochure was clearly meant to satisfy the ego of the founder, rather than actually stimulate new business for the firm. I'll bet it didn't do much in the way of getting sales results, but by giving the boss what he wanted, the marketing executive probably made his own life a lot easier.

That's what I mean by being lazy. We have so much pressure on us to hit those numbers, hit those deadlines, and keep everyone happy that we compromise. Or we want sales results so badly that we take the broadest approach possible to our marketing efforts, hoping to reach as many people as possible with our message.

I call this "spray and pray." You spray your message out there as widely as possible and pray it works. It's the opposite of targeting. It's "broadcasting" in the truest, most literal sense of the word: casting your net as broadly as possible, hoping to catch a lot of fish.

A better approach today is *narrowcasting*—learning as much as possible about your target audience, however small that audience may be, and communicating to them frequently, richly, and relevantly. It's better to reach 10 percent of what I call your "high-potential market" than to reach 90 percent of a market that doesn't really care about your company or your products.

Most readers of this book have probably never done this, so you're understandably a little afraid of this concept of narrowcasting. You don't know how to do it. You don't know how to find the percentage of the market that represents "high potential," and you don't know how to create products, services, or messages that are relevant to that high-potential customer. You're nervous that you'll make a mistake, offend somebody, or look bad to your boss. And let's face it—on top of all that, you're busy! You've got a lot on your plate, and doing thoughtful, careful consumer marketing takes a lot of time. So you continue to "spray and pray" because it's faster and easier. And it's "safe."

But you were smart enough to pick up this book. You know you can, and should, do more to reach new markets. What you may not know is this: *every business can grow this way*. Narrowcasting and marketing to people's values can be your "secret sauce." It will be the thing that differentiates you from your competition and sets you apart in the consumer's mind. And I promise you this: your competitors are not likely to be developing marketing plans around narrowcasting. No, they are much more likely to stick with spray and pray, which means that you have a wide-open field of opportunity before you.

TOYOTA TUNDRAS, NIKE, AND iPHONES

Apple Computers built their business by narrowcasting. In the 1980s, Apple targeted the Macintosh computer at specific, narrow segments like graphic design, education, and publishing. The Mac became the preferred computer for people in those industries. Gradually, the popularity of Macs spread and, today, Apple is one of the strongest brands in the world. The iPhone strategy was similar: they didn't try to sell everyone an iPhone initially. They focused on the people who would influence their friends and colleagues. Apple *narrowcasted* and targeted trendsetters and tech-savvy people who want to stay connected. From there, iPhone sales spread like wildfire.

Jones Soda Company grew their business by narrowcasting, too. Jones Soda Company is a small beverage company, and they never had the multimillion-dollar marketing budgets to compete with established brands like Coke or Pepsi. One of their company mottos is "Run with the little guy . . . Create some change." They want to be seen as the everyman who just happens to make good sodas. This is evident in the witty quotes and unique pictures on each bottle, the fact that they avoid conventional advertising, and their ever-changing flavors.

Because they were a funky "alternative" soda brand, they narrow-casted and went after consumers who might appreciate their funky, small company appeal. They placed their soda coolers in tattoo and piercing parlors, skate parks and surf shops, and funky little fashion boutiques—places that attract people who are into self-expression and alternative lifestyles. They relied on word-of-mouth recommendations from their loyal fans as well as a group of extreme athletes that they sponsored. Today, Jones Soda Company is much bigger and very successful, but they still narrowcast. You'll find Jones in Barnes & Noble bookstores, Panera Bread Bakeries, and Starbucks. They don't just want their consumers to have a soda; they want them to have an experience. By aligning themselves with bookstores and coffeehouses, they are part of the experience the customer has while browsing for books or meeting friends for coffee.

My company helped Toyota launch the redesigned Toyota Tundra in Texas by targeting Hispanic men who work in construction. The Tundra, Toyota's largest pickup truck, faced steep competition from brands like Ford and Chevy, which were perceived to be "tougher" trucks. Toyota needed to establish the new Tundra as the biggest, baddest, toughest, most durable, hardworking truck on the market. Trucks are enormously popular among Hispanic men, and sales research showed us that Hispanic men buy more trucks than any other consumer group. But to truly "narrowcast," we needed to identify *which* Hispanic men would be our best potential customers for the Tundra. In Texas, 74 percent of all construction workers are Hispanic. And if anyone knows about hard work, tough days, long hours, and physically demanding work, it's people who work in construction. We targeted Hispanic construction workers, knowing that if they were convinced the Tundra was tough, durable, and fit their needs, that word would spread throughout the rest of the Hispanic community and we'd be successful. Besides TV, radio, and billboards, our campaign also included using catering trucks, the food trucks that go to construction sites and bring sandwiches and drinks to the workers. We knew we'd have to bring information about the Tundra to the workers, rather than wait for workers to discover the Tundra. It worked. The redesigned Toyota Tundra was a huge success, and Texas was the top market in the country for Tundra sales during the launch.

The key to narrowcasting is to stop thinking about your potential customers with old terminology and concepts. Demographic data (age, sex, income, education, etc.) used to be the main way that advertisers and marketers defined their prospects. But data doesn't tell the whole story of who a potential customer is or what their life is like.

For example, if you wanted to sell peanut butter back when most women were housewives, it was pretty simple. The primary purchasers of peanut butter were (and still are) moms, and they made the decision about which brand to buy: (Skippy or Jif or Peter Pan, etc.). Moms were pretty easy to reach back then. You could build a marketing plan centered on reaching **women, ages 18 to 49.** That's not very specific, but it was sufficient back then. Why? Because ages 18 to 49 are the prime childbearing and child-rearing ages for women. And, since most women then didn't work—they were homemakers—most women had children. Additionally, our culture was different in those days. "Fitting in" and being like all the other moms was desirable. Standing out or being different was usually *not* desirable. So it was pretty easy to saturate the "mom market" just by creating a broadly appealing ad and running it on TV shows that got high ratings among women viewers in the 18 to 49 age bracket. A few well-placed ads in a few soap operas, featuring healthy, happy, adorable kids and their mom making peanut butter sandwiches and—done!

Today, it's different. Women may still be the primary target for peanut butter, but women today are much harder to reach. Most women are moms. Some aren't. Many work. Many don't. Many are single, raising a family and holding down a demanding job at the same time. Some want their kids to eat only organic food or food they've prepared themselves. Others don't cook at all. Some moms value convenience, others, price. You get the idea. Moms are not "one size fits all" anymore.

The point is, demographically defining your customer is not as effective as it once was. It was effective when people lived similar lives and lifestyles, when our culture was more homogenous and when there were fewer media channels. There was a time when there were only three television networks and the news was on just twice a day. Today, we get news instantly, every moment of every day, across every conceivable kind of media platform. We can customize our media choices and choose to receive only the information we want. We can skip past ads on TV and download programs and movies whenever we want. We get everything our way, on our schedule, just the way we, as individuals, want it.

Demographic descriptions don't paint much of a picture of consumers these days. I'm a woman, in that age bracket of 18 to 49. I am completely different than another woman who may be my exact same age and have my exact same household income. I am childless, I live downtown in a major city, I drive a sedan, and I own a business. Another woman my same age may have three kids, live in the suburbs, drive a minivan or SUV, and be a stay-at-home mom. We may share a gender, an age, and even an identical household income level, but after that, we'd have very little in common. My life revolves around work, travel, clients, and marketing. I buy milk once every 10 days. I fill up my car with gas once every two weeks. I meet friends downtown and we go out for sushi.

The mom in the above scenario may have a life that revolves heavily around her kids' school functions, after-school activities, grabbing groceries several times a week, filling up her SUV two times a week because she drives her kids to multiple activities and lessons, and runs a ton of errands. When that mom socializes with her friends, she may be doing it in someone's backyard or at a school function. We're both women, we're both the same age, but that's where the similarities end.

That mom and I are going to have very different priorities. Our lives are completely different. If I see a marketing message targeted to busy moms, it just washes over me and past me because that's not me. I can't relate. The new marketing magic is in creating messages or ads that say "I get you" to your potential customer. "I get you, I get your life, your needs, and your wants, and I have the perfect product or solution for you."

So how do you reach people who are so different? If we can't spray and pray like we used to, what are we supposed to do?

The answer is: dump the demographics and, instead, market to people's *values*. If you can tap into my heart and mind, you'll tap into my values. And if you can do that, you *will* tap into my wallet. It's foolproof.

One of the powerful examples of this is Nike's "Just Do It" ad campaign. Nothing in the Nike ads promised that if you buy a pair of Nike shoes you'd run faster or be a better athlete. They didn't tout the features of the shoes. As an athletic shoe company, Nike knew that people have different reasons for working out. Some people work out to relieve stress. Some work out to control their weight or blood pressure. Some work out because they have sedentary jobs and they crave movement and feeling their body in motion. Regardless of why people work out, everyone's reasons for doing so are personal and valid. Nike perfectly tapped into these values by simply stating "Just Do It." Those three words conveyed so much. They conveyed, "You know why you work out. You know why it's important to you. You don't need us to tell you to do it. You know. So just do it." This spoke to people's *values*, not their demographic profile.

Another example is telecommunications services. Cingular Wireless (now AT&T) was the first to offer "rollover minutes" in one of their plans. The idea came to them from focus groups with young teens, a highly desirable target group because they *live* on their phones. Cingular asked these teens which of their plans they found most appealing: the 2,000-minute plan, the 3,000-minute plan, the 5,000-minute plan, and so on. And the teens in the focus groups responded with comments along the lines of, *"How do I know how many minutes I'm going to need this month? How can I plan to talk 2,000 minutes? Why do the minutes have to expire anyway? Why can't they just roll over to the next month?"* Why not, indeed? And the first plan with rollover minutes was born. It was one of Cingular's most popular plans—*and* one of their most expensive. It was successful, not because it was marketed to a specific demographic group (teens), but because it spoke to that group's *values*. In this case, the rollover minute plan meant "freedom"—it gave the illusion of having the freedom to talk as little or as much as you wanted, because you wouldn't "lose" anything. You wouldn't lose your minutes. And if there's anything teens love, it's flexibility and freedom.

TAPPING INTO THE HEARTS AND MINDS OF NEW CUSTOMERS ALSO MEANS TAPPING INTO THEIR WALLETS

Ultimately, *we all spend money on what we care about*. If you want to learn what people care about, follow the dollars. Look at what people spend their money on, and you will understand what their priorities are.

Do they donate to their church or temple? Do they buy only products made from 100 percent recycled paper and plastic? Do they shop at farmers markets and organic food stores? Do they send their kids to private school? Do they home-school their children? Do they contribute money to charities or political organizations? Do they buy the latest tech gadget the minute it hits the market? Do they save all year to take one great vacation? Do they not save a penny and live in the moment? Do they buy top-of-the-line cookware or eat out every night?

These are just a few examples of how you can study people, what they buy, how they live, and learn about their values. Nothing in the list of questions above has anything to do with demographics. It's all about lifestyles, priorities, and *values*. And that is the secret sauce, the key to how to market to people not like you.

In the next chapter, you'll learn how to research a new customer segment so that you can learn what they might want or need and how you can meet that demand. You'll see how marketing to specific values creates a deep emotional bond between your product or service and your customer. You'll also learn how other companies, large and small, have successfully narrowcasted, gained incremental sales, and grown their business with new and very, very loyal customers.

CHAPTER TWO ⟩⟩

Get to Know the Customer You're *Not* Getting but Should Be

WHO ARE THESE PEOPLE? BABIES, GIRL SCOUTS, AND AMTRAK

In Dallas, we have an art house film theater called the Angelika. They show a diverse mix of independent films and cater to a sophisticated group of film lovers and filmmakers. Now, think about being in the movie house business for a moment: what would be the deadest time of the week for your business? The answer? Mornings. Most movie theaters offer special matinee pricing to lure people to the movies in the afternoon. But no one goes to the movies in the *morning*. Yet, the movie house has everything it needs to have a show: it has the popcorn, the candy and drinks, and the movie itself. The only thing missing is customers.

The Angelika did something about that a few years ago, and it was absolutely brilliant, in my opinion. They were already offering special prices to seniors and students, but realized that there had to be people who just didn't go to the movies, regardless of price. In other words, beyond lowering the price of admission, were there people who wanted to go to the movies, but simply couldn't?

Yes. New moms. Let's face it: just because you're a new mom doesn't mean you no longer like movies, right? The woman who was a film lover before she became a mom is *still* a film lover; it's just that now, she has more responsibility as a new mother and, probably, a whole lot less freedom. The Angelika realized that a new mom has a terribly difficult time getting out of the house to catch a movie. But if there was ever someone who needed a break and a chance to get out of the house, it's a new mom!

Yet going to see a movie poses a dilemma for the movie-loving mom: either find child care while you go catch a film, or take your baby to the movie. Finding child care can really be tough, but if you take your newborn to the theater and the baby starts fussing during the film, the other patrons will give you the evil eye and say "Shhhhhhhh!" It's easier to simply skip the whole thing and stay home. For most new moms, it's just too much hassle to try to go see a movie.

So the Angelika created something just for these film-loving moms: the "Crybaby Matinee." The Crybaby Matinee is offered twice weekly at 11:00 in the morning, timed for baby's first nap of the day. No men are allowed, so that women can breast-feed comfortably. A baby-changing table is provided, so if your baby needs a diaper change, you don't have to miss a minute of the movie. The lights are kept low, but it's not completely dark inside, so that moms can tend to their babies and see what they might need in the diaper bag. The sound is kept a bit lower so as not to harm baby's delicate ears. The Angelika provides "stroller parking" in the lobby. The concept is unique, it's targeted, and it's perfect. It's been wildly successful, too. The women bond with each other and come back week after week. Why? Because they have two powerful things in common: they're new moms and they're movie buffs. What a win-win this is for both the business and the customer. The theater is generating revenue during a time when previously there was none. It costs them virtually nothing to implement this. But it sent a great, targeted message of

"We get you" to these new moms. *"We know you want to get out and see a movie, and we're here to make it a little easier for you."* The program has been so successful that other movie houses and companies in cities all over the world offer similar events. ("Reel Moms" and "Baby Pictures" are just two examples.)

I was speaking at a conference a few weeks ago on the topic of marketing to people who are not like you. I used the example of the Angelika theater to make the point about the best marketing being tailored to the unique needs of the customer you're not getting. A woman came up to me after my presentation and told me that, in her city, there were theaters that now cater to the needs of autistic children: the theater brings the lights *up* and the sound *down* to avoid overstimulating the kids. I was impressed. If you are a parent of an autistic child, why would you go to any other movie house? Clearly, these movie houses have shown respect and understanding of the unique needs of autistic children, and they've tailored the movie experience to provide a great time for both parents and children.

So how do you come up with ideas like that for *your* business? How do you get to know the customer you're *not* getting but should be? What do they need and want?

It starts with identifying who the customer segment is that you're currently missing. Most business owners have a sense of this. They may know, for example, that they're not reaching women or teens or seniors or fashionistas or apartment renters or people who run marathons. Give some thought to this sentence and fill in the blank: *"I know my business could grow if I could just get _____ as customers."*

Usually, this exercise will help crystallize who the customers are that you're missing.

Let me give you an example. In the United States, the Girl Scouts are an organization for young girls to learn skills for success in the real world. The Girl Scouts focus on things like building character, leadership, and other personal qualities that enrich young girls. Every year, the Girl Scouts sell cookies door to door and in public places like shopping centers. The annual cookie sale is almost a sign of spring! Every March and April, Girl Scouts, in their uniforms, suddenly seem to be everywhere at once, selling their cookies to raise money for the organization.

It seems that everyone loves Girl Scout cookies. They have a variety of flavors, and most people have a flavor or two that they like or love. However, despite their success, several years ago, the Girl Scouts realized that they could sell even *more* cookies if they could sell cookies that would appeal to the growing Hispanic population in the United States. To do this effectively, they had to make the cookies appealing to Hispanics. You see, most cookies in the United States are much too sweet for Hispanic tastes. In Latin America, sweets are made with less sugar, and greater emphasis is put on natural flavors like vanilla or cinnamon. So the sweets and treats in Latin America have a much more subtle taste. The Girl Scouts' first Hispanic-targeted cookie was called *Olé Olé*—it was a cookie that was less sweet and a bit drier than most, more like a Pecan Sandy or Walkers Shortbread cookie. Today, the Girl Scouts sell *Dulce de Leche* cookies—they're made with caramel chips and *dulce de leche* is a classic flavor in Latin America.

Amtrak, the only passenger railroad system in the United States, recently began marketing efforts to the gay and lesbian community. "We are always looking for new ways to reach potential passengers, and this community travels a lot," Amtrak representative Karina Romero stated. It makes sense for Amtrak. Gays and lesbians spend a lot of money on travel, and other major companies such as American Airlines, JetBlue, and Expedia are marketing to the gay community. Why wouldn't Amtrak want to get their share of this lucrative passenger market by promoting the comfort and convenience of train travel?

My company has been helping Sherwin-Williams, the second-largest paint company in the world, tap into a customer they hadn't been reaching: Hispanics in the United States. The growing Hispanic population in the United States represents a huge opportunity for Sherwin-Williams to grow their business. Not only are Hispanics buying homes and are, therefore, great "do-it-yourself" painting customers, but many workers in the painting industry are also Hispanic. That means that offices, homes, stores, and schools that are constructed need paint, and these construction contractors, painting company business owners, and workers are all making decisions each day about which paint to buy. To get to know the Hispanic painting customer, we conducted focus group research and learned that what Hispanics value most about paint was "getting the job done right." This gave us great ammunition to build marketing efforts around because that is exactly the key strength that differentiates Sherwin-Williams from its competitors. Unlike home improvement stores that sell paint, along with a million other items, Sherwin-Williams are paint specialists, paint experts. They are completely devoted to paint and coatings, and their employees are the best trained in the business. They are true paint experts. So if you want the "job done right," you're going to get the best advice, products, materials, and help from Sherwin-Williams. We built the marketing messages around this message, and sales to Hispanic customers have increased in the test markets.

Once you've identified who the customers are that you're not currently getting, you need to do a little homework. You'll need to learn about them so that you can figure out what product or service you can offer that will attract them and bring them to your business. Don't guess at this—find out. Here are some ways you can research a potential new market.

GO ONLINE AND READ EVERYTHING YOU CAN ABOUT THE GROUP YOU WANT TO TARGET

A friend of mine is a real estate agent and wanted to reach prospective first-time home buyers. By reading blogs online and spending time in chat rooms, he discovered that prospective first-time buyers are overwhelmed by the process of buying their first home. It's a big step, one that is very exciting, but also very scary because there is so much they need to know. He's in a perfect position to help. He created a free, no obligation seminar to be held in the evenings, called "How to Buy Your First House—the Do's & Don'ts for Getting the Best House and the Best Deal." He promoted the seminars with flyers that are distributed in areas with high apartment rentals. Because who are first-time home buying candidates? Renters! He offered his free seminar in a neutral place, a local community center, not in his office. This made the potential buyers feel relaxed and under no pressure. He kept it short, 60 minutes, because people are busy. And he provided attendees with a list of the key steps needed to make a good decision in buying their first home. Because he did this, he's seen as the "expert," dispensing free advice. Why would anyone do business with someone other than him? He's demonstrated that he's the "good guy" and "he gets them"—he gets that they are nervous and scared of making a mistake. So he gave them his wisdom and advice, and that, in turn, fostered their trust in him. His sales to first-time home buyers grew 60 percent in his first year of using this tactic.

ATTEND EVENTS, MEETINGS, AND GATHERINGS OF YOUR POTENTIAL CUSTOMER; OBSERVE AND TALK TO ATTENDEES TO FIND OUT WHAT'S ON THEIR MINDS

Selling Harleys to Women

This is an excellent "hands on" way to get to know someone who is not like you. If you spend time with people who don't currently do business with you, you're going to learn a lot about them. You'll learn what's holding them back or why they do business with one of your competitors. Let me give you an example of how Harley-Davidson tackled this with a customer segment they wanted to reach: women.

A Harley-Davidson dealer in the Seattle area realized that he wasn't getting many women riders. He knew he could grow his business by expanding into the women's market, but he also knew there must be a reason why so few women were coming to his dealership. He started attending women's expos and talking to women everywhere he went and asking them if they'd ever thought about riding a Harley-Davidson. He found that women were very vocal about Harley-Davidson and motorcycles, and they expressed things like this to him:

- "I'd *love* to have a Harley! But I don't know how to ride."
- "I'd love to ride, but those bikes are so heavy. I don't know if I could handle one."
- "I love the motorcycles, but I love the Harley clothing even more!"
- "I've always wanted to ride a motorcycle, but I don't just want to walk into a dealership when I don't know whether I really want to buy one. I wish there was a way I could "try it out.""

These comments and insights made the dealer realize what was holding these potential customers back: fear and intimidation. He decided to hold a series of free "Rider's Clinics" for women only, on Saturdays. He had a female staff member teach women how to ride. They went over basic safety and riding skills and had an obstacle course where women could practice maneuvers comfortably. The bikes that the women rode were lighter weight and not the heaviest motorcycles. They offered complimentary refreshments. They had a fashion show because the women were just as interested in the Harley-Davidson apparel and leather accessories as they were in the bikes. And you know what else they offered? Free pole-dancing lessons! Yes, that's right. In addition to being able to learn how to ride a motorcycle in a class taught by a woman, and have refreshments and a fashion show, these women could also learn to pole dance at the Rider's Clinic! You may be asking, "What's the connection between pole-dancing lessons and learning to ride a motorcycle?" Well, the dealer was smart enough to realize that the kind of woman who is drawn to riding a Harley-Davidson has a certain kind of *spirit*. She's confident, she pursues her own interests, she has a great sense of humor, and she doesn't take herself too seriously. She has an enormous sense of adventure. She's the kind of woman who would see pole dancing as both fun and funny and might say, "Let me try that." And she'd say the same thing about learning to ride a Harley: "Let me try that." This dealer really got to know his potential customers and why they weren't buying. He created a solution to overcome their reluctance to come to his dealership. And he marketed to their *values:* the sense of adventure and the open spirit of trying new things. Today, 30 percent of that dealer's customers are women.

HOW TO RESEARCH A NEW AND UNFAMILIAR CUSTOMER SEGMENT TO FIND THEIR VALUES, TASTES, NEEDS, AND CONCERNS

Want to know a secret? Want to know how the big companies, the ones with huge research budgets, learn more about their customers and potential customers and what they want and need? *They ask them.* Truly, it's that simple. Sure, they may have many different ways of doing this and all have fancy names: focus groups, qualitative studies, quantitative surveys, ethnographic studies, and more. But the reality is, every one of these approaches comes down to simply talking to people and probing what's on their minds. Big companies that spend a lot of money on consumer research use different techniques to find out what they need to know, but what it all boils down to is asking people what they like, what they don't like, what they wish they had but don't, how they use certain products and services and why, why they like one company over another, and so on.

You can do your own market research, and you don't have to spend a fortune to do it. Let's say you want to talk to teens about your product or service. You could get a group of teens together by posting a flyer at a local high school and inviting them to participate in a panel discussion to give their opinions about certain topics. All you'd really need to conduct your own "focus group" is three things:

1. A place to have the focus group.
2. A small amount of compensation for the attendees. It could be a small gift card or light refreshments (pizza and soft drinks). I've seen focus groups where the participants got a T-shirt and a coupon for a free product. You just want to provide something to the participants that says *"thank you."*
3. A list of the questions you want to ask or the areas that you want to probe. Having a list will keep the conversation on track and ensure that you accomplish your goals.

You can do your own "consumer research" and essentially use the same techniques that big companies do. Remember: people love to give their opinions. And people love to be *asked* their opinions. Get a group together of the potential customers you want to learn more about, and ask them for their candid opinions on your product or service, your competition, your pricing, and so on, and I promise that you will get valuable insights that will help you in your marketing efforts. Ask, ask, ask. Then listen, listen, listen.

LISTEN TO COMPLAINTS

Complaints tell you what people don't like and, conversely, what they do like and want. You can listen to complaints in person or you can "listen" online. When people state what they don't like about something, it instantly tells you what they feel they are missing, and *what's missing spells opportunity*. For example, here are some real comments I gathered from various web sites, blogs, and chat rooms about a variety of different places and products. Next to the comment, I've put the "remedy" or opportunity that is clearly called for.

- "Great restaurant. Too bad they don't serve breakfast." (Open earlier.)
- "I liked this product a lot, but it's too big to put in my purse." (Make it smaller.)
- "This store has great stuff at great prices, but they close at 6pm." (Expand hours.)
- "Great jeans. Wish they came in black." (Expand color offerings.)
- "Love this stuff, but it's so expensive." (Make a less expensive version or a smaller quantity that can be sold for less. Wines do this with smaller "splits"—bottles that have just enough for about one and a half glasses of wine.)
- "You have to buy a membership. Wish I could just pay as I go." (Offer single purchase options at a higher rate, giving a discount for ongoing customers.)

HIRE FROM THE TARGET GROUP, IF POSSIBLE

The best insights into your potential new customers may come from someone just like them. If you want to grow your business with more senior citizens, then consider hiring a senior to advise you or work with you. If you're trying to reach students, another student will have specific and unique knowledge about what students care about and how they spend their time. If you want to cultivate customers from a certain racial or ethnic group, add someone to your team who reflects that group and who speaks the language, understands the culture, or both.

UNDERSTAND THAT THE WAY WE RECEIVE INFORMATION SHAPES US ALL

When trying to learn about a new or unfamiliar group of people and what they might want or need, it's helpful to also understand how they choose to receive information and the way in which information that was provided in their lifetime shaped them. This is most clearly seen in generational differences. For the oldest generation, radio and newspapers were the primary ways that news and information were provided. They had significant limitations: it was one-way communication, and the content was controlled by the broadcaster or publisher. Even the time of day that information was available was controlled. Consequently, those of this generation recall certain "routines" formed around these information outlets. Breakfast was eaten while scanning the morning newspaper, and the family would gather in the evenings to listen to the radio. There was no ability to ask questions about the information, so if you wanted to know more, you had to ask someone or go to the library.

The Baby Boomer generation, those born between 1946 and 1964, had television as their primary source of information. Content was still controlled, but for the first time, people could "see themselves" on TV, and images of collective human clout were powerful and compelling. Suddenly, if there was a protest or a march, you could actually see just how big the crowds were and what the mood was like. This led to Boomers realizing that they could accomplish big things if they worked together.

Gen X, those born between 1965 and 1981, used computers while they were in school or as they were just entering the workforce. For the first time, technology gave consumers a bit of control: you could record TV shows on videotape and watch them later! It allowed you to personalize your experience with media and make it more private. Additionally, cell phones (mobile phones) entered the picture, making everyone reachable at all times.

Gen Y, those born between 1982 and 1994, has had more information in their bedrooms, all of their lives, than is available at any library. The Internet has provided speed and access to information, and, consequently, Gen Y has never had to wait for what they want. The digital world also allows them the freedom and anonymity to express their opinions about everything, and they do.

You can see that the way information flowed to us has changed throughout the years. It's no surprise, then, that different generations may prefer products or services to be provided to them differently. Let's take banking, for example. A younger person wants to be able to do everything himself, at the click of a mouse, in isolation, and at any time he wants. So banks offer online bill paying, mobile banking, and the ability to manage your accounts, transfer funds, and so on, with no help from a person at the bank.

My mom, who is in her 70s, would much prefer to go to the bank, have a live conversation with a teller, make her deposit in person, and receive a paper receipt for that deposit, which she will then file when she gets home. In these scenarios, both customers want very different things from the same bank, and both of their needs and wants are perfectly valid. Furthermore, the bank is never going to get my mother to do her bill paying online. Nor are they going to persuade a young person to go into the bank every time she needs to conduct a transaction. The bank has to adapt to the different customers, rather than expecting the customer to adapt to the bank's offerings.

HOW TO HIRE A MARKETING OR ADVERTISING CONSULTANT WHO UNDERSTANDS THE TARGET GROUP YOU WANT

If you feel that you need more help to effectively reach a new and unfamiliar prospective customer, you may be more comfortable hiring some professional help. There are marketing and advertising professionals who specialize in "niche" marketing, whether it's racial or ethnic marketing expertise or tapping into specific market segments. Here are three tips for hiring competent help in this area:

1. *Determine whether you need help with advertising or whether you need help that is broader than that.* Ad agencies are adept at making ads and commercials and placing those ads where your potential customers will see/hear them. An ad agency may not be able to assist with larger, strategic issues like whether you have the right product offerings or packaging, or cultural insights or how to get involved in the target community at a grassroots level. If you need more than advertising, you're better off looking for a marketing professional.

2. *Ask for referrals.* If you know anyone who is working within the target customer group you want to reach, ask them if they know people who specialize in professional marketing for the group or customer segment. Chances are, they may know someone you should talk to, or at least with whom you can network. Let's say, for example, you want to reach restaurant owners. You could attend some professional meetings of restaurant owners and ask members of that organization if they know of companies that specialize in marketing within the restaurant industry.

3. *Access professional directories and associations.* Virtually every industry has a professional association. These associations are

formed to provide ongoing education and assistance to their members. As such, these associations often have lists of resources for their members, and these lists may contain key contacts of marketing professionals or companies that specialize in a specific area. For example, suppose you want to market your product or service to hair salon owners. There are several professional associations, and even state and local chapters of many of these types of organizations. Explore the associations and you'll often find a directory of professional resources—companies that provide specific services to that field or industry. This can be an excellent way to find qualified help for specialized marketing efforts.

You've now identified a customer that you're not currently getting but should be. You've educated yourself about this customer and you've learned what they do and what they like. You've familiarized yourself with their values, tastes, and concerns, and perhaps you've even added someone from this target customer group to your team. You've explored using outside professional marketing help, if needed.

You're now ready to look at your product or service offerings, because that is a crucial step in marketing to people who are not like you. The next chapter focuses on how to tweak your product or service to be relevant to a new customer group.

CHAPTER THREE ➤➤
What Do They Need?

Tweak Your Product or Service Offerings

Now that you've identified the customer you're not currently getting and you've become more familiar with who they are and what their tastes, values, and concerns might be, it's time to look at whether you may need to modify your product or service offerings. Tweaking your products or service may better meet the needs of these potential customers and attract them to your business. Additionally, it communicates, in a clear and tangible way, that you are actively reaching out to a new community of customers. It communicates a strong message of validation, and what customer doesn't want to be validated? We all want validation. We all want respect and we want businesses to appreciate us and the money we choose to spend with them.

How does modifying your product offerings communicate that you value a customer and want their business? Fresh, innovative products or services that "speak to you" convey three powerful messages in a subtle way:

The first message that is communicated is "I see you." This recognition is the first step in validation. No one likes to feel overlooked, invisible, or as if they're not important. The fact that, as a business, you see and recognize a new customer group conveys a message of respect. It says to the consumer, "You're here and you're important. You matter. What you think matters, what you want matters, and where you do business matters. Please do business with me."

The second message that is conveyed is "I value you." We feel valued when we know that someone has gone to some special effort for us. After all, when someone fusses over you or makes extra effort to take care of you or do something for you, it's because you are important to them and they want to please you. It communicates that you are *worthy* of extra time or attention or a specific product development or modification. So when you see a product that you know has been made "just for you," you respond by feeling a connection to that brand or product. It may not happen on a conscious level, but it does happen. Take toothpaste for children, for example. Toothpaste used to be marketed to families, and let's be honest—kids probably don't really need special toothpaste just for them. But kids like cool things; bright, shiny things, and colorful things. So the toothpaste manufacturers created toothpaste with sparkles in it. Brightly colored sparkles appeal to kids. It's more "fun" to brush your teeth with sparkly toothpaste! And even though the sparkly toothpaste costs a little more, parents buy it because, if their child likes it, maybe they'll brush their teeth a little bit longer or more thoroughly. Brushing longer is not a bad idea, so what the heck—the sparkly toothpaste goes in the shopping basket.

The third message that is communicated by offering different or modified products or services is "I want you." I want your business. I want you to spend your dollars with me, and I am inviting you to do so. By offering something just for you, something that I think you'll like and that will be helpful or meaningful to you, I am letting you know that I want you as a customer. I am "putting the welcome mat out" for you.

You may be asking yourself how you're supposed to tweak your products or services to attract new potential customers and meet their needs. The best way is to take an honest appraisal of your business offerings and ask yourself if what you have is what the new customer group actually wants. Let me give you a few examples:

REAL MEN EAT SALAD

There is a funky little restaurant near my home called Greenz. It's a place that started out serving exclusively salads. In fact, their tagline is "Salads for Z'adventurous." It's a terrific little place owned by a woman who has a great eye for taste combinations and upscale offerings. The salads are gourmet: unique flavors, beautifully presented, and a few are downright exotic: warm pear and goat cheese, edamame and wasabi peas, chipotle—you get the idea. In this part of town, the residents and workers are pretty fashion conscious and figure conscious, so a salad restaurant is a smart business concept. I live just a few blocks from this eatery, so on many nights, I've stopped in and picked up a couple of salads to go. One night, I came in to place my order to go and, as I was waiting for them to be prepared, I started chatting with the owner. The restaurant had been open for only a few months, and I asked her how her business was going. She replied, "We're doing great with women, we're always packed at lunch with women, but we're just not seeing a lot of men. I hope we'll be able to attract more men as time goes on." I didn't give her comment much thought at the time. After all, it's a *salad* restaurant. It didn't really surprise me that she would attract more women patrons than men. In my experience, women tend to choose salads more frequently than men do.

Several weeks later, I was in Greenz again, and once again I found myself chatting with the owner, killing time while I waited for my salads to be prepared. I asked her how the business was doing and told her that I recalled that she'd said they didn't have many men patrons. Her response floored me. She said, "We do now! We figured it out! Our salads were too "girly" for most men. Too fussy and light. We figured that men may want something a little more substantial. So we created a new salad with men in mind. This salad is made with sliced steak instead of sliced chicken, and it features roasted nuts and is tossed with a wheat-beer vinaigrette. And it's served in a pretzel bowl!"

"A pretzel bowl?" I asked. "What's that?"

"You know what a taco salad is, right?" she asked. "A salad served in a taco shell bowl. When you're done with the salad, you can break apart the taco bowl and eat the taco chips. Well, we created a bowl made from pretzel! It's thick and has the salt crystals on it and every-thing. When you're finished eating the salad, you just break it apart and have pretzel for dessert!" she said proudly. I complimented her on her innovative idea and told her that guys must love it—it sounded like just the kind of salad a man might find appealing. She confirmed that, yes, men did indeed love the salad and were flocking in every day for lunch in numbers she hadn't seen before. But the best part was when she shared a customer comment with me. She said that one of her new "regulars," a guy who came in at least twice a week, always ordered the pretzel salad and told her, "I love this place! Feels like bar food, but it's good for me!" *Bar food.* Pretzels and nuts and steak and wheat-beer vinaigrette. Absolutely brilliant.

The greatest thing about this little story is that the owner of Greenz is not a marketing professional. She's a restaurant owner. She's a smart woman who figured out that there was an entire market segment she wasn't getting (men) but should be. She was able to honestly assess why she wasn't getting them. (Her salads were too "girly.") She modi-fied her product offerings and "put the welcome mat out" for men with a special salad created with them in mind. Sure, anyone can order that salad, and I'm sure many women do, but its primary "target customer" is a man, and the strategy is working. You can almost hear the conversations that must take place between women and men about Greenz: "Honey, let's go to Greenz tonight for dinner."

"No, that place is too frou-frou. I want something more than just salad for dinner."

"They have a new one called the "Bar None"; I think you'd like it. It's got steak, roasted nuts, a dressing made from wheat beer, and it's served in this cool pretzel bowl."

"Really? OK, that sounds pretty good. Let's go."

A good business owner, in touch with her business and the customer she's *not* getting, expands her customer base solely by add-ing a targeted new product to her offerings. Great "tweak"!

Even companies as large as McDonald's tweak their product offer-ings. In South Texas, where the Hispanic population is a significant part of the total population, you can get *jalapeño* added to your hamburger for just a few extra cents. In India, there are no Big Macs because Hindu people do not eat beef. Instead, they have the Marahaja Mac, made of lamb or chicken. In parts of Canada, you can order the McLobster lobster roll. In Japan, the menu offers Ebi-Filet-O (shrimp burgers) and green tea–flavored milkshakes. In Greece, you can order a Greek Mac, a burger made of patties wrapped in pita. And in Germany, McDonald's serves beer!

SHOP AT SAM'S, GET A LOAN

Sam's Club, a division of Wal-Mart, is "tweaking" its products offer-ings by offering loans up to $25,000 to small-business members. Sam's Club says 15 percent of its business members reported they had been denied business loans due to tighter lending practices among traditional banks. The Sam's Club loans are focused on businesses owned by minorities, women, and veterans. Wal-Mart and Sam's are retail stores, but they are growing business by "tweaking" their prod-uct offerings to meet the needs of their customers. In this example, the tweak is leading them into the financial services industry.

TARGET IN EAST HARLEM

A competitor of Wal-Mart is Target, and they, too, tweak their prod-uct offerings to appeal to various customers. Target's first store in Manhattan is in East Harlem, a very diverse neighborhood. The mer-chandise has been tailored to the customers; Target offers Spanish-language greeting cards, multicultural dolls, religious candles, per-sonal care items geared for black and Hispanic people, and renowned Southern food that is produced locally.

NO BIFOCALS FOR ME, THANKS!

The eyewear industry is on a roll these days. Why? Because the Baby Boomers are aging and most people need glasses for reading as they get older. So that means that millions and millions of people who never used to wear glasses are now wearing them. But the industry has had to offer a new product that, until this generation started turning 50, had never really been needed before: the bifocal lens with no visible sign of the change in the lens. In the past, reading glasses all had the little "half moon" lens imbedded in the glasses. Baby Boomers associate reading glasses with "getting old," and they'll wear glasses as long as there's no "half moon" that indicates that they are *reading* glasses. Not only did the eyewear industry respond and tweak their products with the invisible reading lens, they charge a significant premium for the lens! And the Baby Boomers happily pay it.

MOVING MOM AND MAKING IT EASIER

Sometimes the product you offer is actually a service. And modifying the services you offer to capture new customers can be very lucrative. I was a speaker at the American Moving & Storage Conference a while back and, at that time, their industry was hurting. Corporate relocations were down overall and the budgets for the relocations that were being made were considerably tighter, forcing everyone in the industry to keep prices low. The moving business is a tough one, even in the best of times. Most people who are moving or relocating are under a lot of stress, and moving is a hassle. It's expensive and not very pleasant. Consequently, the moving industry is not one that most people have a tremendous "bond" with. In fact, most people choose a moving company largely based on price. Sure, service plays a role, and if you're moving, you want to use a reputable mover so that you have confidence that your belongings will be safely transported and not be lost or damaged in the process. But once you find a few reputable movers, you will typically get several bids and, at that point, price becomes very important in the decision-making process.

For moving companies, this is bad news. Because if you position yourself as being low priced, someone can always beat your price. It's a very vulnerable place to be and certainly not a very profitable place to be. How can you make more money or increase profit if you're constantly forced to cut prices to stay competitive?

At this conference, I learned of a privately owned, small moving company that was having its best year ever, in terms of both revenue and profit. I spoke with the owner of the company and asked him what he was doing, what his "secret sauce" was that was helping him to have his best year ever. Here's what he told me:

He stated that while corporate relocations were his "bread and butter," he thought he should be able to do more business locally and wondered what kind of customer would pay for his services. Not students—they don't have enough money and they have too few belongings. Not families—he was already doing a good business with those who move locally and many have lots of friends and relatives who help them move, so they don't necessarily need a moving service. Then he realized his own life was presenting an opportunity to him. You see, he had an elderly mother who lived alone. She was suffering the early stages of dementia and could no longer take care of herself. She needed more care than he could provide, so he made the difficult and heart-wrenching decision to move his mother to an assisted-living care facility. As much as he knew in his heart that this was the right decision, it was still very emotional for him and he felt very guilty. His mother had lived in her home for more than 40 years and didn't want to move. All her memories were there. Everything she felt comfortable with was in that home. She cried and told him she didn't want to move. That only made the sense of guilt he was feeling even worse.

When moving day came, he had an idea. He realized that his mother felt "uprooted" and that the new place she was going to live would be unfamiliar and, therefore, scary to her. He took digital photographs of every room in her house and made special note of the placement of her belongings in every room. They packed her things, moved her to the assisted-living facility, and when they unpacked her items, they used the photos to replicate everything, as best as they could, in every room. If her previous home had an end table with a lamp on it and a framed portrait of the grandchildren next to the lamp, then they put that same lamp and photo on the end table in her new little apartment. This gave his mother a tremendous sense of familiarity and comforted her during a stressful transition. It also made the moving business owner feel a little bit better. He realized that there wasn't much he could do about the whole unfortunate situation, but he could do this one thing for his mom.

He then realized that millions of people face this same difficult situation every week and every month, and he realized that he could offer this special service at a premium price. Instead of just selling "packing and transportation," and trying to be as competitive as possible on price, he was now selling a "Special Senior Services" package that included photographing a home and placing items in the new residence accordingly. What he found was that because this situation is very emotional, people are willing to pay a premium for a service that helps ease the difficulty. He focused on a new customer: *people with aging loved ones*, and he marketed his company and his service as being sensitive to the needs of the elderly. He needed no extra equipment or training for this service. He didn't have to revamp his primary business. He still does lots of corporate relocations and local moves. It's just that, now, he's added in an entirely new revenue stream that he didn't have before and one that is highly profitable. He hit upon a great idea, based on the unique needs of a customer he wasn't getting. And as our population continues to live longer than any previous generation, there will likely only be more demand for his service as time goes on. Again, simply brilliant.

Sometimes tweaking your product offerings to attract new customers means creating a new company or brand. Toyota did this when they created the Scion brand. Toyota found that younger people did not identify with the Toyota brand. Although they were familiar with the brand and even held it in high regard, it was seen as their "parents' car" and therefore, not "cool." Toyota wisely created an entirely new lineup of vehicles that were priced at an entry-level, low price to attract young buyers. Called Scion, the vehicles were sold exclusively at Toyota dealerships and they were deliberately manufactured "bare"—they weren't loaded up with lots of bells and whistles and accessories. This allowed the young Scion buyers to customize their vehicles without making the car so expensive that it was out of their price range. Toyotas all looked the same to these young buyers. They wanted something distinctive. They wanted something no one else had. By buying a Scion and then "tricking it out" with custom accessories, they had a unique vehicle that no one else had. It was a win-win for Toyota/ Scion dealers, too: accessories are highly profitable, and most dealers make more money from the sale of the accessories than they do from the sale of the vehicle itself.

Soma Intimates is another example of creating a business to cater to a new customer. Soma Intimates sells lingerie and undergarments for women who are in their 40s to late 50s. As the Baby Boomers age, women are finding that some of the other retail stores that specialize in lingerie no longer meet their needs. These women don't wear many thongs and bikini panties. They don't need or want a tiny, lacy bra. Their bodies are changing, and what they want is comfortable, practical clothing that still looks pretty. Soma Intimates caters to this customer. Their product offerings consist of panties and bras and lingerie that is touted as "comfortable and designed to flatter every body." To my knowledge, no one has paid any attention to the lingerie needs of the older woman. Soma Intimates said "I see you" to the middle-aged woman and put the welcome mat out for her. This woman has lots of money to spend, and I'm betting she's spending a sizeable chunk of it with Soma.

You can see how just tweaking your product or service can target an entirely new customer group. And you can see how creating a new product or service offering can expand not only your customer base, but your sales and profits, too. People will pay a premium for what they want. Talk to people, using the research approach in Chapter 2 to find out what people want. Then use your products to meet those needs and give people what they want, and in so doing, you will validate them and make them feel welcome in your business.

In the next chapter, you'll learn how to "put the welcome mat out" at your business to make new customers feel special and that they've come to the right place.

CHAPTER FOUR ➤➤
Make Your Sales and Customer Service Friendly

Little Things Make a Big Difference

At this point, you've identified a new potential customer group that you're not currently getting. You've done your homework and researched their needs, tastes, values, or cultural habits. You've taken a good look at your products and services, and you've tweaked them to meet the needs of this customer segment. You're ready to go, right? Time to start advertising and get the word out and make some money, right?

Not so fast. There's another very important step in marketing to someone who is not like you, and that is operational readiness. It can make the difference in whether your efforts succeed or fail. It can not only help bring new customers to your business, it can help retain them. In fact, it's so important that, if I had to counsel a client on whether to focus on operational readiness or marketing, I'd advise them to tackle operational readiness. It has the potential to do more to help your business grow with new customers than marketing can.

OPERATIONAL READINESS—THE "SECRET SAUCE" IN MARKETING TO PEOPLE NOT LIKE YOU

Once you've got the right product for your new potential customer, you're ready to bring them in for business. But what will the experience be like for them to do business with you? Is your business really set up to handle the particular needs or demands of the new customer? If not, then trying to conduct business with you will only make the customer frustrated and they may not return. Worse, the new customers may even tell others not to do business with you. Some great ideas and marketing campaigns have stumbled or even failed because of lack of operational readiness.

Excuse Me, This Bag Doesn't Have a Handle

An example of this is the Container Store. It's a store that sells everything you could ever want to meet your storage needs. Their products are cool, clever, colorful, practical, and innovative. When you go into the Container Store, you'll find "storage solution" products for problems you didn't even know you had! And no matter what you need to store, wrap, hide, stack, or organize, they have it.

They opened a flagship store in Manhattan a few years ago, their first store in New York. It was a fantastic idea to open a store there. After all, people who live in large, crowded cities like Tokyo, London, and New York never have enough storage space. Closets and cupboards are small, and space is at a premium, so being efficient and organized is imperative.

The Container Store quickly realized three things they hadn't thought of in doing business in New York:

1. Their shopping bags needed handles. New Yorkers walk everywhere, so when they shop for items, they need to be able to carry them home easily, and bags with handles are a necessity.

2. They needed to provide delivery service. Manhattanites are used to everything being delivered, and they don't mind paying for delivery, even on inexpensive items. Since most people who live in the city don't have cars, they have their larger purchases delivered.

3. Manhattan customers change their minds—a lot. They'll plan an entire closet system in white and then decide they want it in platinum. The Container Store needed an inventory and software system that could accommodate combinations of transactions that most systems could never handle.

In this example, things like delivery service and having shopping bags with handles are part of being operationally ready. For the Container Store, these were eye-opening customer issues that had been overlooked. The executives had to learn how people who reside in large cities live and shop. In doing so, they learned that their *operations,* not their products, had to be tweaked.

It's all about making sure that doing business with you is *easy.* There are many choices for consumers these days. Lots of choices mean that customers can be selective. And when customers can be selective, they'll do business with those companies that make it easy, fun, or rewarding to do so.

In Chapter 2, I highlighted the Angelika theater's Cry Baby Matinee as an example of reaching out to a new customer segment— in that case, new moms. From an operational readiness standpoint, if you're going to attract new parents and babies to a movie theater, you'd better have a place for the parents to leave their strollers, and you'd better have a place for them to change diapers. These are operational concerns. They have nothing to do with the product that is offered, but everything to do with whether you can actually handle the new customer you've worked so hard to get.

Another example is Mattress Firm. Mattress Firm is the largest mattress retailer in the United States. They have hundreds of stores all across the country, and their sales teams are among the best trained in the industry. The company places strong emphasis on training their associates because the purchase of a mattress is not only expensive, it's one that most people undertake only once every 10 to 15 years. Sleep habits are highly personal, and in order to sell you the right mattress for your particular needs (back problems, soft or firm preferences, etc.), they take a very consultative approach to customer sales.

In Phoenix, Arizona, Mattress Firm chose to test a new initiative targeted to Hispanic customers. At the time, about one third of the Phoenix population was Hispanic. Of the 120 Mattress Firm employees in the market, only six spoke Spanish. The six bilingual employees were constantly being called upon by the non-Spanish-speaking employees to assist in sales. The sales associates were all compensated by commission, yet the bilingual employees who assisted in making a sale for another employee didn't receive any compensation. This led to a group of associates who were highly skilled and in demand because they were bilingual, yet they were demoralized because when they helped their coworkers, they didn't make any money. They felt taken for granted and overlooked.

The customer experience wasn't great either. Think of it from the customer's viewpoint for a moment: you walk into a store to look at mattresses and a sales clerk goes to the phone and starts dialing. Who are they calling? The police? Immigration? You can see what an awkward situation this could potentially be. At the very least, it's not a warm, welcoming environment. At worst, it's insulting or downright scary.

To correct this awkward, uneven process, Mattress Firm held an all-employee meeting and announced that they would be changing their business approach in Phoenix to test a new process. The first thing they did was create a weekly schedule of when the six bilingual employees were at work. They made sure there was always coverage—that more than one bilingual associate was always on duty.

The second thing they did was create a simple card in Spanish. On one side of the card, it stated, *"Hello! I don't speak Spanish, but I am going to call an associate who does. While I reach them, will you please fill out the back of this card so that we may better assist you?* On the back of the card, in both English and Spanish, were a series of questions and boxes to check. Are you looking for a king, queen, full, or twin-sized mattress? How did you sleep last night? Do you have any back problems? Neck problems?

The customer would fill out the card, the English-speaking associate would call one of the six Spanish-speaking associates, and then the English-speaking associate would tell the Spanish-speaker what the customer was looking for. The phone was then turned over to the customer, and the Spanish-speaking associate took it from there. It wasn't a perfect system, but it *was a system*. For the first time, the associates had a process and knew what they were supposed to do.

The third thing the company did was change its compensation plan to split the commissions in these situations so that both sales associates earned commission from the sale. It was a win-win for all parties involved: the customer received help in Spanish, the English-speaking associate now had a system to follow and a way to communicate with a customer with whom they couldn't previously communicate, and the Spanish-speaking associate felt valued and fairly compensated for their contributions. The employees enthusiastically embraced the new system, and Mattress Firm saw a measurable lift in sales among Spanish-speaking customers.

Operational readiness can mean different things for different companies and different customer targets. It might mean having someone on your staff who speaks the language of your customer. It may mean having signs in your place of business that offer policy information or other information in another language. It may mean accommodating the physically challenged. Frost Bank is committed to serving deaf and hard-of-hearing customers. Their operational readiness efforts called for partnering with Deaf Link to provide American Sign Language translation services. Frost Bank also provides agreements, checks, and other documents in large print for customers who have difficulty reading small print. When looking at your business through the "lens" of your new potential customer, ask yourself this: What are all the areas of business, all the departments and processes that a customer in this group will encounter? Are we set up, across all these areas, to serve this customer?

A great example of operational readiness for a specific customer group is Freedom Paradise. This is a resort that caters to large-size people. Their marketing tagline is "Live Large. Live Free." Large and overweight people represent a sizeable percentage of the population. And they have money to spend on vacations. The problem is, many large people don't feel comfortable putting on a swimsuit and hitting the beach. At Freedom Paradise, everything is scaled to the large-sized guest. The doors are broader, outdoor lounge chairs are wider, the beds are sturdier, the towels are larger, the hammocks are super-sized, the pools have sturdy steps instead of flimsy aluminum ladders, and the showers in the guest rooms are huge. The resort even offers a secluded beach to protect guests from the stares that they are often subjected to on public beaches. "It's not a hotel just for large people. It's a size-friendly place where anyone can enjoy a holiday," said owner Jurrian Klink, a Dutchman who thought up the idea while observing the behavior of overweight guests at his former hotel. "What we noticed was that a lot of oversized people don't feel comfortable at resorts." In addition to providing the physical comforts for large-sized guests, the resort also employed operational readiness techniques in other ways. Staff members of all sizes were hired and trained in "size-awareness issues," and low-fat menus were developed for guests who wished to watch their weight. Optional exercise classes were designed by Kelly Bliss, a fitness guru specializing in workouts for the plus-sized. Even the outside firms that the resort partners with had to be on board: for example, the company that the resort uses to teach scuba diving to guests offers wetsuits in extra large and extra-extra large sizes.

OPERATIONAL FRIENDLINESS

Friendliness Costs Nothing and Means Everything

In addition to being operationally ready, it's imperative that your business also be operationally friendly. What is operational friendliness? It's "putting the welcome mat out" for your new customer and making them feel like they are in the right place. It's making them feel welcome and special and as if you really value their business. In the case of Freedom Paradise, none of their terrific efforts to be operationally ready would mean a thing if the staff made plus-sized guests *feel* uncomfortable. Operational friendliness is about being aware of how your target customer *feels*. It's about making every effort to make sure your external efforts to get that new customer are backed up with an experience that the customer will value. Much of it has to do with staff training and being sensitive to the needs of your potential new customer. Can you imagine if you saved all year for your vacation, went to Freedom Paradise expecting a size-tolerant environment, and found that the staff snickered about your size or stared? You'd feel as if you'd been deceived. That's why operational friendliness is so important.

NEW HOURS, NEW UNIFORM

Sometimes, the way you can show your operational friendliness is subtle. A few years ago, I met an independent insurance agent in Omaha, Nebraska, and he had his operational friendliness down to an art form. He is a white man, and not Hispanic, but he speaks perfect Spanish because he was raised in Mexico City. As a business-man in Omaha, he saw the growing Hispanic population in the area and realized that there were very few, if any, insurance agents target-ing their marketing efforts to the local Hispanic population. He created marketing plans in Spanish, and, of course, Spanish-speaking customers started coming almost immediately. But he noticed some-thing right away. He noticed that many of his customers seemed to be uncomfortable in his office. They seemed rather shy and reluctant to come in. This was a problem because selling insurance is so personal and everyone's needs are different. It requires extensive one-on-one conversation between the agent and the client.

He thought about what might be holding his potential customers back, and he realized it was his office and his own appearance. As an insurance agent, he'd been taught that it was very important to portray a serious image, one of stability and success. After all, finan-cial services are about money, and money is a serious topic. So his office had a mahogany desk and plush carpets, and every day, he came to work wearing a suit and tie. But these very "symbols of success" made his potential customers feel awkward; many were working-class men who labored in jobs like painting and construc-tion, and they would come to his office straight from work. Their clothes and shoes were often dirty, and they felt self-conscious about "making a mess" in the agent's office. Rather than communicate strength and stability, the fancy office and the agent's attire was *intimidating and made the customer feel out of place.*

Within two weeks, the agent replaced the carpeting with tile floors that could be easily cleaned, and he replaced his expensive mahogany desk with a sturdy metal desk. He also stopped wearing suits and ties, opting instead for khaki slacks and a collared polo shirt. He expanded his hours into the evening because many of the laborers worked as long as there was daylight, and they didn't finish work until 8:00 PM or later. So three nights a week, he kept evening hours, staying open until 10:00 PM to meet with potential clients. His ability to speak Spanish made him operationally *ready*. His office and his appearance made him approachable and operationally *friendly*.

Perhaps one of the most remarkable examples of operational friendliness is Morgan's Wonderland, the world's first theme park for disabled people. From an operational readiness standpoint, it offers everything that you would expect such a park to offer: wheelchair-accessible rides and swings and the ability to accommodate anyone with a disability. But it's the little things that make it so operationally friendly and special: the staff receives sensitivity training and background checks, there is a garden sanctuary if a child needs a break from overstimulation, and the exits are all secure. Advance registration is required, so that the park does not become overcrowded and therefore overwhelming or upsetting to guests with disabilities such as autism. And admission for those with a disability is free. One guest, a parent of an autistic child, said his daughter enjoys repetition, such as playing on the seesaw over and over. At Morgan's Wonderland, such repetition doesn't cost more. The infrastructure of a park like this must demonstrate operational readiness for its guests, of course. But not charging guests for repeated rides shows a real connection with and understanding of whom the guest is and what they want and need. *That's* operational friendliness.

DO THE EASY THINGS FIRST

You might be asking yourself just how to get started in making sure your business is operationally ready and friendly. Start with the easy things first. If you need to hire someone from the target group so that you can better understand the customer, do that at your earliest opportunity. Look at your product offerings through the lens of your target customer and see what adjustments you can make that would make it easier for them to do business with you. A small, local sporting goods store owner told me about how he noticed that his foreign-born customers tried on soccer jerseys numerous times. Why? Because

CLOTHING SIZE CHART						
COUNTRY	AUSTRALIA	US	UK	ITALY	JAPAN	FRANCE
XXS	6	0 - 2	6	38	5	34
XS	8	2 - 4	8	40	7	36
S	10	4 - 6	10	42	9	38
M	12	6 - 8	12	44	11	40
L	14	8 - 10	14	46	13	42
XL	16	10 - 12	16	48	15	44

SHOE SIZE CHART					
AUSTRALIA	ITALY	US	UK	JAPAN	FRANCE
5	36	6	3	22	37
5.5	36.5	6.5	3.5	22.5	37.5
6	37	7	4	23	38
6.5	37.5	7.5	4.5	23.5	38.5
7	38	8	5	24	39
7.5	38.5	8.5	5.5	24.5	39.5
8	39	9	6	25	40
8.5	39.5	9.5	6.5	25.5	40.5
9	40	10	7	26	41
9.5	40.5	10.5	7.5	26.5	41.5

NOTE: Shoe sizes on the website are italian unless otherwise stated

IMPERIAL & METRIC CONVERSATIONS											
INCHES	26	27	28	29	30	31	32	33	34	35	36
CENTIMETERS	66	69	71	74	76	79	81	84	86	89	91

FIGURE 4.1   International Sizing Chart

American sizing is not the same as international sizing. His customers didn't know what size jersey they wore in U.S. sizes. So he posted an international sizing conversion chart in the soccer area of his store (see Figure 4.1). His customers were able to easily find the correct size jersey once they knew what size to convert to.

Think of operational readiness as the cake. Operational friendliness is the frosting that makes the cake taste really good. If your customers experience both operational readiness and operational friendliness from you, they will keep coming back for more.

Once your business is operationally ready and friendly, you're ready to take the next step. In the next chapter, you'll learn how to communicate in a relevant manner, by showing respect for other cultures, values, languages, and priorities.

CHAPTER FIVE ➠
Communicate in Their "Language"

Develop Marketing Messages Based on Their Values

OK, so far, you've identified the customer you want but haven't been getting; you've learned as much as you can about them and what they want, need, and care about. You've tweaked your product or service, if necessary, to meet their needs. And you've made sure that your business is operationally ready and operationally friendly for this new customer. Now it's time to actually communicate with them.

In this chapter, when I talk about communicating in someone's "language," I don't necessarily mean a foreign language. If your potential new customer speaks a language other than the one you've been doing business in, then, of course, you'd want to market to them and communicate to them in their native tongue, if possible.

What I mean by communicating in "their language" is making sure that your message has *relevance* to your new customer target. Your message must be authentic and sincere. It must reflect that you understand this customer and that you are reaching out and inviting them to do business with you.

There are several ways to communicate with relevance. One is with the native language of the potential customer. Suppose you've been doing business all along in English, but you really want to reach Canadians who speak French. After you've researched the market, you would probably add someone to your staff who can speak French. This would undoubtedly help with day-to-day business issues—everything from sales to customer service to marketing. Once you have your French-speaking team member hired, and you've made your business as operationally ready and friendly as possible for those who speak French, you're ready to let your target customer know that you want their business. So you create ads in French and place them in the areas, publications, and places where French-speaking Canadians are likely to see them. The very fact that you are marketing to these consumers in their native tongue is a huge "welcome mat." In this case, ads in French would convey, "I know you speak French, and we do, too. We want your business and we're ready to serve you—in French."

A note of caution here: if you market to someone in their native tongue, it implies that you are *ready to do business in that language*. It implies that you are set up to do business with someone who speaks that language. It's not hard to understand why that would be so. Suppose you own a small local restaurant and over the years, you've noticed that the community around your restaurant has changed and there are more Vietnamese people living and working in the area than ever before. You want to attract these residents and workers to your restaurant, so you research Vietnamese food and drinks and you make some modifications to your menu. You add Vietnamese coffee to your beverage offerings and lettuce wraps to your appetizer selection. You then hire a translation company to help you translate your marketing messages into Vietnamese, and you place flyers in the high-density Vietnamese neighborhoods and at the Vietnamese grocery store, and you also take out an ad in the local Vietnamese newspaper. (In almost every community, as immigrants arrive, so does media that serves that immigrant community.)

And guess what? Vietnamese patrons start coming to your restaurant! But when they get there, no one on your staff can serve them very effectively because no one on your team speaks Vietnamese! You can see from the customer's viewpoint how this would seem weird, if not outright misleading. After all, you created ads in Vietnamese for them and placed them in their community and in the newspaper they read or on the radio station they listen to. When they went to your restaurant, they had every reason to expect that someone would be able to help them in Vietnamese, so it's surprising, frustrating, and disappointing to learn that wasn't the case. It was presumed, and logically so. It was presumed because you put the welcome mat out *in Vietnamese.*

Therefore, *don't market or advertise in another language if you have no ability to actually do business in that language.*

A second way that your message can be relevant and reflect your target customer's "language" is through cultural relevance. Cultural relevance means reflecting a group's *values.* It means showing that you understand the unique needs of a group and that you respect their values. Let's say your business is day care for children. Chances are, many of the parents of the children that you care for have to work every day. That's why they need day care for their children—because the parents work, either full or part time. And let's suppose that the majority of your children are picked up by these working parents by 6:00 PM each day. As a small business owner, you see no reason why there shouldn't be a way to expand your business into the early evening, thereby increasing your revenue. You're willing to stay open until 8:00 PM, and you even have an employee who has expressed interest in working later hours. You ponder what types of parents need child care in the early evening. Suddenly, you hit on an idea: offering a "play group" to children who are home-schooled! Home-schooled children need activities with other children, to form important interactive skills and develop social skills in general. Many parents who home-school their children have conservative and specific religious views, and they won't necessarily be keen on letting their children play with other kids who don't share their values. So an organized play group for home-schooled children has lots of potential.

You decide that a few nights each week, from 6:30 to 8:00 PM, you will offer play groups for children of different ages who are home-schooled.

Now you're ready to create a message to the home-schooling community about your new service. You want it to reflect the values of the parents and be culturally relevant. So you create flyers and posters that promote your play groups and what they feature. Perhaps you develop games that have lessons in them that support certain religious teachings. Or perhaps an activity offered is singing Christian or Hebrew songs. Perhaps activities include biblical plays and reenactments. You get the idea—your message must speak the "language" of the parents, in this case a conservative or religious message that will appeal to parents who are trying to instill certain values in their children. By communicating in this way, you're not only showing the potential customer "I get you," you're showing them "I respect you." You're communicating that you understand where they're coming from, what they're trying to do, and that you have a service that fits in with their life and their *lifestyle*.

Another example of "speaking your customer's language" might be with certain words or phrases that communicate that you see these potential customers, you understand them, and you have something that they need.

Let's go back to the example of you as the restaurant owner. Let's say that, instead of targeting Vietnamese customers, you want to target people who exercise. Near your restaurant, the city has just put in a running and biking trail, and now you have hundreds of people who use the trail daily and who pass very close to your restaurant every day. What an opportunity! So you modify your business to be operationally ready for these customers by opening for breakfast. This allows you to reach the morning exercisers. Then you tweak your "product," adding smoothies and whole-wheat toast to the menu, as well as egg-white omelettes. You're ready! You want these customers, so you advertise on a billboard near the parking lot where the trail begins, and your message reads: "Refuel" and features a delicious-looking smoothie on it. The billboard states that you're open at 6 AM and serve "healthy breakfasts as well as home-style breakfasts" (something for everyone). You have posters made with "Refuel," and those go in the window of the restaurant, where passersby can see them clearly. By using the same "language" that athletes use ("refuel"), you are showing them that you see them, you respect what they're doing (taking care of their bodies), and you have products that fit into their lifestyle (healthy smoothies, etc.). You're speaking their "language," and they will gravitate to your restaurant because of it.

A third way that you can communicate with relevance is through style. The use of slang or specific words can be highly meaningful to certain groups. Take the word *cool,* for example. Teens have always had words that convey "cool," but the words change all the time. The words that teens use today will not be the word in use tomorrow. As of this writing, the word *sick* is popular among teens as a synonym for something really cool; for example, "That song is so sick! I love it!" Other popular terms are *sweet, tight, off the hook, raw, über,* and *wicked.* Years ago, it was *rad,* as in "radical." The hip-hop music industry has many words that are unique to it: *def, phat,* and others all mean "cool." By using certain words in your message, you communicate to the people most likely to use those same words—you are speaking in their "language."

TRANSCREATION, NOT TRANSLATION

Suppose your target customer does speak a language different from your own. To communicate most effectively with this customer, you'll probably want to take a good look at creating marketing messages in their native language. How do you do this? Most people think that simply translating a message from one language to another will do the trick. But there's more to consider. There are times when it makes sense to translate, and there are times when you must "transcreate." Let's define them so you understand the difference.

To "translate" something means to take a phrase in one language and replicate it in another. Any message that is created in one language and needs to be conveyed in another language must be translated. Translation works well when there is little or no nuance to a message, when what you are communicating is very black and white and there is no "interpretation" of the message. Here are some examples of phrases that can be easily translated:

- Open Monday through Friday
- We accept Visa and Mastercard
- Exit here
- Now serving beer and wine
- Two forms of identification are required

You can see how there is no cultural "nuance" to any of the above phrases. These are phrases that can easily be translated into any language. Most translations are almost "word for word," meaning that the very same words used in one language are used to express the same message in another language. For example, "free photos" in English translates to "fotos gratis" in Spanish. The same words (*free* and *photos*) are used in each language, and the meaning is the same.

To "transcreate" means that you express the same *meaning* of something in one language, but not necessarily word for word or even close to that of the first language. Transcreation is called for in any of the following situations:

- When the phrase in one language is meaningless in another language
- When the phrase in one language in unfamiliar or confusing in another language
- When a phrase does not have cultural relevance in another language or culture

Let me give you a few examples of each. In all of the following examples, I will use a primary phrase in English and show how and why it must be transcreated into Spanish.

When the Phrase in One Language Is Meaningless in Another Language

Every culture and language has idioms and phrases that are widely used and understood. However, when those idioms are translated, word for word, into other languages, they often lose their meaning and become nonsensical. For example, a common phrase in English is "the bottom line." This phrase has several different meanings in English: it can mean "in summary" (*the bottom line is that we'll be hiring*

100 more workers); it can mean "profit" (*the revenue went straight to the bottom line*); and it can mean "lowest possible cost" (*we went all the way to the bottom line to get this account*). However, in Spanish, there is no such expression as "the bottom line" at all. If you were to translate the phrase, it would read "la linea baja" (the line below), but it would be an utterly meaningless phrase. It would be as non-sensical as saying something like "girl tree happy" in English. They are English words, but put together, they mean nothing. So if you had a marketing message in English that stated, "The bottom line is that no one beats our prices!" you'd have to have that *transcreated* rather than translated. It would be necessary to communicate the same thing, but use different words. In Spanish, a transcreation of that could be "garantizamos nuestros precios" (we guarantee our prices). Even though the word *guarantee* was not used in the English phrase, by stating that "the bottom line is that no one beats our prices," the guarantee is implied. After all, if no one can beat your prices, then you are guaranteed to have the lowest prices, right?

Here is another example from translation work we do for Popeye's Chicken & Biscuits. They had a promotional offering not long ago for a choice of three chicken strips, three whole wings, or three pieces (leg, wing, and thigh). The headline for their promotional posters was "3 of a Kind." This phrase ("of a kind") does not exist in Spanish, and a literal translation, "3 de un tipo" (three of a type) does not make sense in Spanish. We *transcreated* the message as "Lo Mejor Viene en 3" (The Best Comes in 3s). You can see that this is far from a literal translation, but it communicates well what the offer is: a promotion centered around three items.

When the Phrase in One Language Is Unfamiliar or Confusing in Another Language

There are times when a phrase that is familiar or common in one language is confusing in another. An example in English, in the United States, is "lower 48 states." This phrase refers to the 48 states in the United States, excluding Alaska and Hawaii. In Spanish, this phrase "lower 48 states" would be unfamiliar at best, and confusing at worst. To transcreate this phrase, clarification would be needed as to which states are included or excluded in the "48."

Another example might be a phrase like "the alarm went off." Technically, the alarm went "on," right? It's a strange phrase, even in English, because we use the word *off* but actually mean that it went "on." You can see how this would be a phrase that would need to be transcreated rather than simply translated. You'd need to communicate that the "alarm was ringing," not that it was "off."

When a Phrase Does Not Have Cultural Relevance in Another Language or Culture

Just because a phrase has *meaning* in another language does not mean it is *relevant*. An example of this was when a bank asked us to translate their marketing brochures from English to Spanish. They had brochures for each of their products, which were varying types of accounts (checking, savings, etc.) and loans. They had brochures for home loans, auto loans, home improvement loans, and personal loans. In their brochure for personal loans, the brochure in English stated, "Why would you want a personal loan? For that motorcycle or RV you've always wanted to buy."

We know that Hispanics (who were the target of this bank's marketing efforts) do not index high in the purchase of motorcycles or recreational vehicles. So while we could have easily *translated* that copy, we chose to *transcreate* it instead, and we wrote for them (in Spanish): "Why would you want a personal loan? For that family vacation you've wanted to take or that family computer you've wanted to buy." These examples were more relevant than motorcycles or RVs, and, therefore, the communication was more meaningful. Even though the phrase is different, it communicates the same type of *reasons* why someone would apply for a personal loan.

I've used English and Spanish examples in this chapter to illustrate situations that call for transcreation instead of translation. But make no mistake—*every* language has certain phrases that just don't work in other languages. So whether you need to create messages in French, Chinese, Spanish, Italian, English, Vietnamese, Greek, Hindi, Farsi, or any other language, be aware that you'll probably have to go down the transcreation road at some point.

How can you know whether your message needs to be translated or transcreated? There are two ways to approach this. If you hire a translation service to translate your message, be sure and talk with them about transcreation. Let them know that you are interested in the most relevant, meaningful communication of your message, and ask them to work with the message and copy with that in mind. Be aware, however, that most translators are not copywriters. Translation services are best used for simple messages with little or no nuance to them. And here's a note about how translation services typically charge: they usually charge by the word for the number of words in the finished, translated language (not the original language).

To get a good transcreation, you'll probably need to work with a marketing firm or ad agency that specializes in the language you need. It's not hard to find such companies on the Internet, and most of them offer translation/transcreation services. These companies typically charge by the hour, so ask them if they'll provide a free quote on how much it will cost to transcreate your document. You may pay slightly more for a marketing firm or ad agency to do transcreation for you, but it's usually worth it because your message will be much more effective.

TWEAK YOUR MARKETING, ADVERTISING, SIGNAGE, AND WEB SITE IN OTHER LANGUAGES

With the diversity that surrounds us, all around the world, it's a good idea to provide information about your company, your products, your areas of specialty, your personnel, your hours, and so on in another language (or languages), if that makes sense for your business. In other words, if you're a small business owner doing business locally and you see that your local community has a large and growing Asian or Hispanic population, you'd be wise to prepare your marketing materials in the relevant language of these growing populations.

This can seem daunting. You may be asking, "Where do I begin?"; "What will this cost?"; "Do I need to translate everything I do?" Don't be overwhelmed. Take it one step at a time. If the majority of your business is conducted over the Internet, it makes sense to start there. And while it may be cost prohibitive to redo your entire web site in another language, it's usually pretty inexpensive to just add an "FAQ" (frequently asked questions) page in another language. Even an FAQ page in another language is a big step toward "putting the welcome mat out" for new customers. The type of information that you could include on a simple FAQ page may be things like your hours, your products, your location and contact information, and the names and photos of any employees who speak that language (so that the customer can call and speak with someone if they have questions).

If you primarily work with local customers who come to your store or site (or you go to them), it's best to start with the most important communication pieces first. For example, Home Depot and Target now have bilingual (English/Spanish) signage in almost all U.S. stores and certainly in all of their stores in high-density Hispanic areas. Being able to find the lighting section or the bath section in large stores like those is important, so the stores have signage that helps both English-speaking and Spanish-speaking customers navigate the aisles and merchandise.

If you primarily use brochures or other collateral pieces to help you sell, then start by having those pieces translated or transcreated first. Every company, big and small, that has identified that there is opportunity with customers who speak other languages has had to go through this process. You're not alone. Just take it step by step, starting with the most critical elements of your business that customers use or see, and build from there. Be patient—you *will* see results.

"BUT THIS IS AMERICA—SPEAK ENGLISH!"

Why should you have to translate anything at all? You don't. There is no obligation on any business owner's part to put the welcome mat out for customers in other languages. But it's the smart thing to do. Because the reality is, technology makes it easier than ever for people to stay in touch with their loved ones all over the world and to receive news from all over the world, in any language, at any time. Consequently, it's easier than ever for every person to live comfortably in their language of preference. This is fact, and this will not change.

There's a business opportunity out there for you with new customers, some of whom (or many of whom) may speak another language. These consumers have money and may want and need what you have to sell. In fact, they will do business with someone—it might as well be you. If you don't want their business, trust me—someone else does and will make it easy for them to do business in their language of preference.

If you wait for them to learn your language and come to you, ready to do business in your language, you may well miss out on a tremendous amount of business and revenue. You are certainly entitled to feel any way you want to about whether people should speak your language or not. But the reality is that many don't. And your feelings won't change that fact.

Marketing is not about dealing with the world the way you want the world to be. It's about dealing with the world *the way the world is.*

This is business. The simple question to ask yourself is, "Do I want to grow my business with new customers, some of whom may not speak my language?" If the answer is yes, then the steps outlined in this chapter will help you do that. There is significant money to be made and tremendous business and financial opportunity for you, both now and in the future.

CHAPTER SIX ▶▶
Use Technology to Reach Your Prospects

Micro Targeting

It's an exciting time for marketing now. Why? Because there have never been so many low-cost and no-cost options for marketing and so many exciting new avenues for business owners and marketers to explore. In the past, you had to have a marketing or advertising budget to get your message out to your target. And even when ads were placed in newspapers, magazines, on TV or radio stations, or on billboards, they weren't nearly as targeted as today's media allows us to be. Technology is your friend when it comes to marketing. It allows you not only to reach more of the "right" customers for your business, but to learn more about them and to harness their input and feedback to make your business and your products continuously better. In this chapter, you'll learn tips for using technology to reach customers who are not like you.

USING FREE OR INEXPENSIVE ONLINE TOOLS

1. Create Your Web Site and Keep It Up to Date

Every business should have a web site now. There is no reason not to have one. It's a mandatory. People search for what they need by going online, and you can't be found if you are not there. It's called "shelf consideration"—how can I choose a brand of toothpaste I want to buy if my store doesn't have it on the shelf? The same principle applies here: if I am looking for information about a product, brand, or service, I am going to look online, and if you're not there, I can't choose you. So it starts with having a web site that features all the information that a potential customer might want to know about you.

Make sure your web site works properly, too. It's astonishing to me how many businesses have sites with broken links or outdated information. Updating your site is simple and shouldn't take much time or money. Your site is the single greatest source of advertising and marketing you have, so make sure it reflects the best of your business. Make sure all the information you have on it is current and interesting and that no links are broken.

Here's another tip: don't misrepresent yourself. I know a marketing consultant who operates his business from his home, as so many do. He's a one-man shop and has been in business for several years. On his site, he has an option for "About Us." When you click on that button, it takes you to a few more options, one of which is "Our People." The problem is, when you click on "Our People," expecting to see a list of the professionals on his team and perhaps their bios, the page features just him. There are no "people"—there is only one "person": him. There's nothing wrong with being the only person in your company. But if that's the case, don't misrepresent yourself on your site. It's not professional, and it's also very transparent to the reader what you're doing—you're trying to look bigger than you are. But by not having anyone else on the site in the section called "Our People," you're actually calling even more attention to the fact that you work solo. Just be yourself and let your work speak for itself. That's what your customers are most interested in anyway.

Your web site is commercial. Its function is to tell your customers and prospects what they need to know about you to entice them to do business with you. Here are some of the things that your web site should include, if possible:

- Complete contact information, including a way that someone can contact you directly from your site (a link that allows them to e-mail you)
- Your hours, or hours of customer service, if not 24/7
- Your products and services, featuring the most popular ones
- Your prices or fees, if applicable
- Customer testimonials from satisfied customers
- Awards and/or accolades, if any (either for your company or your products; e.g., "Named Best Plumber in Vancouver!")
- Your experience or credentials, including bios, training, and certifications for you or your staff, if applicable
- Helpful tips, comments, or facts that would be of interest to the customer. Some sites have a "tip of the week" or "tip of the day" to keep customers coming back on a regular basis.

Make your web site as good as you possibly can. Make it as thorough and complete, as relevant and as appealing, as possible. The people who will visit your site are *already interested in you*. Make sure that once they've landed on your site, you give them a good reason to stay and browse and learn about you. Think of it this way: someone visiting your web site is essentially "standing at your doorway, trying to decide if they want to come in." Make it irresistible for them. Make them want to come in and look around and see all that you have to offer. If you follow only one recommendation from this chapter, make it this one. Your web site is your business, and there is no excuse for having a sloppy, broken site.

Once your web site is where it needs to be, you have the foundation from which you can build many other forms of customer communication. It's important to have your web site in top shape because that is where all other forms of communication will drive your customers to. Whether you send out e-mail blasts or newsletters or cultivate an active presence with social media, your customers will ultimately be fed back to your web site for more information or to do business with you.

2. Create a Database and Maintain It

Building a database is the logical next step in developing your electronic communication "arsenal." Your database should, at a minimum, contain all of your customers, past and present, active and inactive. Most businesses already have a customer database, so what you'll need to do is extract the e-mail addresses and create a list of just e-mail contacts.

If you don't have any customers yet, if you're just starting your business, then build your database with every contact for whom you have an e-mail address. This list can include friends, colleagues, associates, vendors, and acquaintances. The larger your database, the more you'll find that e-mail communication will work for you. This is because of two factors: the sheer statistical return and "pass-along readership." The statistics for e-mail marketing conversion vary by industry, but a good rule of thumb is to use 0.3 percent. That means that if you send out an e-mail blast to 1,000 people, you're likely to get 3 people to act on that e-mail (call, purchase, subscribe, or whatever your offer or invitation was for). Therefore, the larger your database, the more sales you'll likely make.

The second factor is pass-along readership. This means that someone in your database receives your e-mail offer and forwards it on to someone else. That new person may never have heard of you or your company, but because they were referred by a friend or someone they trust, they are very, very likely to open that e-mail and read it. Chances are, they may respond to the e-mail with an inquiry or a purchase, because someone who knows them thought that your e-mail would be of interest to them.

Every time you meet someone or exchange contact information, add them to your database. It costs you nothing to do so.

3. E-mail Marketing

You can now begin to use e-mail blasts to communicate announcements, special sales, product launches, limited time offers, almost anything you can think of. Just be sure that each e-mail communication has relevance: what's in it for the reader? Will the information in the e-mail save your customers money? Will it make them more knowledgeable or better informed about products or services? Does it offer tips for them that will save time, money, or hassle? Does it alert them to upcoming changes in your policies or procedures? Make sure that every e-mail communication is focused on "what's in it for the customer." For example, let's say you are an upscale local grocer who sells hard-to-find, specialty meats and produce. Let's say that your local community newspaper has just named you "The Best Gourmet Food Store." This wonderful accolade is really something to be proud of and you frame the article and hang it on your wall for all your customers to see when they come in the store. But you want everyone to know about this honor, so you send out an e-mail blast, announcing the accolade and include the article in which you were featured. While many of your customers may be happy for you, many others will read this, shrug, and go on with their day, because there was nothing in it for them. If, however, you included a large offer at the top that stated, "Thanks for helping us be the Best Gourmet Food Store— please enjoy 20 percent off your next purchase with this coupon." You've announced your news, but you've also made this e-mail blast highly relevant. Your recipients now get an exclusive discount of 20 percent on their next purchase. This will stimulate traffic and sales and your e-mail announcement will be much more effective.

Everyone gets too much spam these days. The way for you to make sure that your e-mail communications are viewed as valuable and not as spam is to keep the customer in mind at all times. It's OK to brag about yourself or your company or your accomplishments—just make sure there's something in it for the reader as well. Usually, that means a special offer of some kind.

E-mail blasts are inexpensive and effective. And all e-mail communication should direct the reader back to your web site or to your phone number. There should always be a "call to action" in your e-mail communication.

4. Newsletters

The same database that you use for e-mail marketing can be used to send out newsletters. Newsletters are a great way to keep your customers and potential customers up to date on what's new with your company or products and they can be as short or as lengthy as you like. Now, you might be thinking, "Where am I going to find the time to write a newsletter? And how will I put it together?" Good questions.

First of all, you don't have to write 100 percent of the content of the newsletter. Some of the best newsletters feature headlines of relevant, interesting articles written by someone else. The newsletter may highlight the headline and first paragraph of the article and then offer a link to the full article. This is a great way to provide your readers with content without having to spend hours developing the content yourself.

For example, let's say you own a backpacking tour guide company. You take small groups of people on hikes through the Swiss Alps. Your newsletter could feature an article on "What to look for in waterproof boots," an article you found online. This would be a great article for your customers to read because it's written by a third-party expert and it's highly relevant to someone who is likely to go hiking in the Swiss Alps. In this case, all you'd have to do is use the headline and entice the reader with an opening sentence or paragraph and then provide the link to the original article you found online.

What about the actual creation of a newsletter? What's the best approach to creating an attractive, easy-to-read and easy-to-assemble newsletter? There are numerous services that are very user friendly and very low cost that you can subscribe to. Each offers a variety of newsletter templates, so that you can create the format and style that best meets your needs. Here is a list of some of the best or most widely used newsletter services:

- Constant Contact (ConstantContact.com)
- Vertical Response (VerticalResponse.com)
- Jango Mail (JangoMail.com)
- EmailSynergy Platform (EmailSynergy.com)
- Easy Contact (EasyContact.com)
- iContact (iContact.com)
- Contactology (Contactology.com)

- MyEmma (MyEmma.com)
- Mail Chimp (MailChimp.com)

The largest and probably best known is Constant Contact. A real up-and-coming one, which is known for how easy it is to use, is MyEmma. But all of these (and others) can get you started with creating good-looking, professional newsletters that will reflect well on your company.

The best newsletters stay focused on customers and what may be most meaningful or helpful to them. In our earlier example of the local, upscale, gourmet grocer, a newsletter would be the perfect place to feature recipes and cooking tips. Of course, the recipes would feature ingredients you would find at the store! For tips, the newsletter could feature "secrets from the chef," highlighting a different chef each time, perhaps with a different area of specialization.

This leads us to another way to expand your low-cost and no-cost ways to use technology to reach potential customers: linking to other businesses with whom you don't compete.

5. Link Exchange

There are many businesses that you don't compete with, but that are very compatible with yours. These compatible businesses are an opportunity for you to expand your online marketing presence among potential new customers at no cost to you. Let's say you own a tire store. You sell and install tires for every type of vehicle there is. Every day, you have cars and trucks up on lifts as you install tires. While you are working on your customers' autos, suppose you notice that some of them need new mufflers. You don't sell or install mufflers, but you know of a great service mechanic just down the street who does. He does fine work and has a great reputation. This would be an ideal match for link exchange. Because he doesn't sell tires and you don't sell mufflers, your businesses don't compete. Yet you share a common customer type: one who takes care of their vehicle and one who will pay for professional installation of tires and mufflers.

In this example, you could ask the owner of the muffler shop if you could add his web site link to your e-mail and newsletter marketing and also to your web site. This is a win-win for all parties: your customers and readers get a link to another service they may need at some point and the referral came from you, so they will trust your referral. The muffler shop owner is getting additional exposure at no cost. And you're getting additional credibility with your readers because you are demonstrating that you are a "resource" for their needs, not just trying to sell them tires today. With link exchange, the muffler shop owner would also include your web site link on all of their communication too, so you'd benefit from the additional exposure to their database as well. It's like doubling your database.

When considering other companies with whom to do link exchange, make sure that their professional reputation is as good as yours. You want to associate with companies or organizations that have the same standards that you do when it comes to things like product or service quality, customer care, business practices, and so on.

Another terrific benefit of link exchange is how it increases your rank among search engines. And this leads us to discuss search engine optimization.

6. Search Engine Optimization (SEO)

When someone searches online for a company, or product information, they use "keywords" in a search engine, such as Google or Yahoo. With online searches, your goal should be to increase your "ranking"—where your business and information appears on a search page after the user has typed in a keyword. Let's say you're looking for a carpet cleaning service. If the user types into Google or Yahoo "carpet cleaning," more than 11 million responses can be displayed. If your business is listed on page 875 of the search, no one will find you. So you need to make sure that your site is optimized for search engines—this will increase your rankings and make your site more readily "found" online.

The more refined keyword searches yield better results. For example, if you had an ad agency, it's unrealistic to try to achieve a top ranking with the keyword "advertising"; there are billions of searches for this word every month. But if you select a keyword phrase that more specifically describes the nature of your business ("health advertising," for example, is a phrase that is searched only a few thousand times each month), then the search will be substantially narrowed and your results will be greatly improved.

There are some free tools that let you test potential keyword phrases and that will then suggest others you may not have thought of. On Google, you can find this tool by searching "Find Keywords." Yahoo offers a similar tool. Wordtracker.com offers a modestly priced, online keyword development system as well as a seven-day free trial.

Here are some resources for getting started with SEO:

- "Search Engine Optimization Made Simple" at About.com
- "Search Engine Optimization Made Easy" at easywebtutorials.com
- "Easy Search Engine Optimization, Non-Technical Steps to Optimize Websites and Increase Search Traffic" at website-marketing .suite101.com.

7. Social Media—It's About People, Not Logos

Perhaps the most powerful tools online are the social networking sites: Facebook, LinkedIn, etc. For most businesses, Facebook is the preferred place to focus efforts and cultivate fans. Facebook is the largest social networking site in the world and it's one of the easiest to use. For personal relationships on Facebook, you have "friends." If you have a business page on Facebook, you cultivate "fans," people who "like" your business.

As a business, you want "fans." Fans are those who like, or even love, your company, your products, and your services. They are genuinely interested in your business. Being a "fan" allows them to stay up-to-date on what's new with your company. It also allows them to talk to you and you to them. The dialogue takes place online, but it's real and offers a more human, personal, "social" side to your company or business.

The biggest mistake that business owners make when creating a social media page (such as a Facebook page) is that they try to replicate their web site. They put all the information that's on their web site on their social media page. That's a mistake because the reason that people use Facebook and sites like it is not to be sold anything. It's to engage in conversation and dialogue. Jay Baer, a social media marketing expert, states in his presentations, "When thinking about the phrase "social media," drop the word *media* and you'll be on your way to understanding how it works. It's social, folks. You are socializing with your customers, not pitching them."

Think of it this way: imagine Facebook as a "backyard barbeque." You wouldn't go to a casual barbeque expecting to get a sales pitch on a product or service, would you? In fact, it would really be a turn-off if that happened. You go to a barbeque expecting to socialize with people you know and like, maybe meet some new people, learn a few things, and get caught up on what's new with everyone. That's what your business page on a social networking site needs to offer: a friendly, warm conversation that is relevant to the reader without being overly commercial, pushy or a sales pitch. Jay Baer also states, "It's about people, not logos." If people *like* you, they'll *trust* you. And if they trust you, they'll *want to do business* with you. So keep your Facebook page personal, real, helpful, and focused on what your readers and "fans" will find relevant.

A terrific example of this is Bubbles Car Wash. Bubbles Car Wash has thousands of fans on Facebook. Their fans adore them, not just because of the quality of their car washes, but because they provide cool tips for being green, how to maintain your vehicle, do's and don'ts for washing your car, and so on. There's no sales pitch—Bubbles uses their Facebook page to inform their customers and fans about helpful hints and what's new. Their page has suggestions for getting pollen off your vehicle, how to increase your car's resale value and other helpful information. This free, helpful, customer-focused information positions Bubbles as the car wash expert, so why would you have your vehicle washed anywhere else?

Having a social networking site will lead fans to your web site, where you can ask them to sign up for your newsletter or be added to your database. These e-tools all work together to provide multiple touch-points for you to interact with your customers and potential customers. Just remember: it's about people, not logos. Make your social networking page (on Facebook or any other site) feel like you're talking to someone at a backyard barbeque and you'll start to grow your fan base and your customer dialogue.

Technology is your friend when it comes to marketing to someone who is not like you. Use technology to research your customers and their likes and dislikes, to communicate with them, to form relationships with them, and to retain them. Now, more than at any other time in history, it's possible and relatively easy and inexpensive to reach out to a new customer target with the help of the tech tools outlined here. With a little time and effort, but very little out-of-pocket expense, you can create ways to grow your business with people who are not like you.

8. Mobile Marketing—It's Versatile, Inexpensive, and Here to Stay

Our mobile phones are our computers. There's an app (mobile phone application) for just about everything these days. Integrating mobile marketing into your marketing plan can be highly effective and very inexpensive. It's also highly relevant to young and tech-savvy shoppers; these consumers value speed, efficiency, and access to immediate information in ways that fit into their lives.

One of the best examples I have seen of effective use of this technology is by AutoTrader.com. AutoTrader.com is a complete resource for auto shopping. Whether you want to buy a new or preowned vehicle, do research on various types of vehicles, find out what your vehicle is worth, or calculate a payment, AutoTrader.com is a one-stop, comprehensive resource for buying, selling, pricing, and getting advice on the purchase of a vehicle. The company initially started as a weekly publication that featured preowned vehicles in most markets in the United States. As the company grew, and as technology allowed consumers to search for vehicles online, AutoTrader evolved into AutoTrader.com. The online site has every conceivable kind of information that someone in the market for a vehicle could possibly want.

AutoTrader.com is focused entirely on making it easy for consumers to find the right vehicle—the right price, the right equipment, color, features, and so on. The company takes language preference into consideration too: recently, AutoTrader.com launched AutoTrader Latino to make it even easier for Spanish-speaking consumers to find the vehicle and dealership that's right for them. On top of that, research shows that Hispanics use mobile technology more than non-Hispanics, so AutoTrader Latino developed a total mobile marketing strategy so Hispanic consumers could access information in the format most relevant to them.

To be truly helpful, and therefore, relevant, to their consumers, AutoTrader Latino provides auto information in just about any way a shopper wants to access it. A weekly print magazine, an online web site and a mobile site allow shoppers to access information in whichever format they prefer. Their mobile strategy includes iPhone and Android apps, as well as text messaging features. And their use of mobile technology isn't just about sending ads to prospects—they use mobile technology to *make it easier for shoppers to find what they need.*

For example, each vehicle featured in AutoTrader Latino has a unique text ID code that a shopper can type into their phone to receive more information. The shopper is then sent a text message response that connects them instantly to the mobile web site, which features more details about the vehicle and about the dealership. The shopper gets information that is relevant to them, they get it in the way that they prefer (on their mobile phone) and it's fun and convenient. They even market in a clever manner: "Take us from your PC to your pocket." That's smart because when someone is out looking at vehicles, they're going to want information at their fingertips. They need to be able to have the latest information in a mobile format. Her Below are just a few of the features that their mobile products offer and how they market it.

On both the AutoTrader.com and AutoTrader Latino mobile web sites, you can:

- Search for new, used, and certified cars in your area, from both dealers and private sellers
- Contact a seller by phone or e-mail directly from a vehicle listing
- Map local dealerships, and view their services and amenities
- Create a free MyAutoTrader.com account
- Save cars and searches of interest with MyAutoTrader.com, so you can access them from any other mobile device or computer
- Use your MyAutoTrader.com account to easily reference your past saved cars and searches while you're on the go

As a result of this integrated strategy, AutoTrader doesn't just help auto shoppers. The company also helps auto dealers by offering a complete and innovative way to reach viable prospects: in print, through the weekly catalog, online or by mobile web site, in both English and in Spanish. For every way a consumer would want to search for vehicle information, AutoTrader is there. And the results are impressive. AutoTrader's site traffic has grown to over 2 million users per month. More than 200,000 consumers have sent text message requests for vehicle information to AutoTrader Latino within the last 8 months alone.

This strategy has helped AutoTrader deliver value to thousands of auto dealers, resulting in continued revenue growth for the company. Their sales are soaring and it's because they have been a leader in technology that benefits their customers and is relevant to their lifestyle.

You can incorporate mobile marketing into your marketing plan by using text messaging or by placing ads on mobile sites. For example, suppose you have a river-rafting company. You could advertise on sites that have mobile applications for weather. When you pull up the weather app, you'll also see an ad for the river-rafting company with a "click to call" feature and a link to the "specials of the week." Or suppose you have a microbrewery. You want to target sports fans and entice them to stop into the microbrewery after the game for a nice, cold beer. You buy a mobile ad on a local sports mobile site, and when someone is checking the scores, they see an ad for your featured beer at half price, today, after the game.

Mobile marketing is highly relevant as people use their phones more and more for every type of transaction. It doesn't cost much to use this marketing method. Just be sure to have a specific offer and a way for the consumer to respond, whether it's a phone call or a link to your site. Mobile messaging works best with retail offers that have a strong, limited-time, call to action. A good company that I recommend for mobile marketing is LSN Mobile (www.lsnmobile.com). They work with projects and budgets of every size and can give you good information on how best to approach your prospects with mobile messaging.

Technology is a great way to reach people who are not like you. It can be inexpensive and highly effective in bringing new and different customers to your business.

But what if your employees or your core customers don't like that you're marketing to new and different customers? In the next chapter, we'll address this and how best to handle it.

CHAPTER SEVEN ➤➤
Deal with Naysayers

What If Your Employees or Your Core Audience Don't Like Seeing Their Product Marketed to Other Groups?

SUBARU AND DENTISTS

Subaru is an automobile company that is known for making dependable, quality, precision-engineered vehicles. They're kind of a quirky car company; their vehicles aren't necessarily the most stylish or best looking. They're not a status symbol brand. Subaru is also one of the smallest auto companies. In Canada and the United States, they don't sell millions of vehicles; they sell a few hundred thousand. Subaru just makes really good vehicles, and they last a long time. Their owners are very loyal, and many say they wouldn't drive anything else.

Subaru is a company that fully embraces the philosophy of marketing to people who are not like you. In fact, this marketing strategy helped save the company from extinction in the United States and Canada. In the early 1990s, Subaru sales plummeted and the company was on the brink of going out of business in North America. The executives were desperate to make sales. In what is now seen as a major turning point for the company, the marketing team there started analyzing all the owner data they had, poring over every single profile of a Subaru owner, trying to figure out if there was a common thread among them. What they found was astonishing— and useful. They learned that the majority of Subaru owners fell into one of five groups:

- Engineers
- Nurses, physical therapists, and emergency medical technicians (EMTs)
- Teachers
- Outdoor enthusiasts (especially those who enjoy solitary sports like canoeing, kayaking, cross-country skiing, and hiking)
- Gays and lesbians

Armed with this information, and realizing that a small car company such as theirs could not possibly compete in the advertising market against giants like Ford, General Motors, Toyota, and Honda, Subaru made a bold move. They reworked their marketing budget and focused solely on these owner groups. They realized that, with their limited budget, it was smarter to try to reach their high-potential buyers than it was to "spray and pray." They set about crafting highly targeted, very focused marketing plans for these diverse customer groups.

Subaru allocated about 3 percent of their total advertising budget to the gay and lesbian market. Despite that small sum, their dealers were concerned, apprehensive, and vocally opposed to it, initially. No auto company had directly targeted the gay and lesbian market before. It was a big step, an unconventional one, and, certainly, a controversial one. The Subaru executives knew that many of their dealers would be uncomfortable with the direction and decision. But the executives were also in survival mode and so were the dealers. They needed to do something to keep the company alive.

Subaru armed their dealers with the facts and held meeting after meeting to help them understand the strategy, why it was essential, and how to handle any negative feedback they might receive at their dealerships or in their communities. Initially, the dealers were skeptical, and some were outright opposed to marketing to the gay and lesbian community. But when the marketing strategy began to work, when more and more customers started coming into their dealerships, when their sales grew faster than they ever had before, and when these new customers then brought in additional business through referrals, the dealers changed their tune. They realized that their business could survive and even *thrive* with the loyal customers they were reaching in the gay and lesbian community.

Yes, some of the dealers received phone calls from people who thought it was terrible to actively court the gay and lesbian community. Some conservative religious people and groups even boycotted Subaru because of their targeted strategy. But sales went *up*, not down. In other words, despite the fact that Subaru may have lost a few customers who chose not to buy their products anymore, they gained many, many *more* customers who responded enthusiastically (and loyally) to being recognized and targeted. Within a year, even the most skeptical dealers had to admit that the marketing plan worked and their businesses were back on solid ground.

When you've identified a customer group to target that you know will help your business grow, stay the course. There may be those who will question your decision or vocally criticize you if they don't like the group you're targeting. But business is not about appeasing others. It's about growing sales. No one knows your business better than you do. No one should tell you who to target or who not to target. It's about growing sales, and you should put your efforts into reaching those customers who represent your best opportunity to do that.

In Subaru's case, the resistance and nay-saying came from within— it came from the dealers within their own organization. What should you do when someone from outside your company expresses that they don't support your new marketing approach?

About a year ago, I was speaking at a conference for the dental industry. The topic I was speaking on was diversity marketing. An attendee came up to me afterwards and wanted to share his story with me. He's an African-American dentist with a practice in Atlanta, Georgia. Atlanta happens to be one of the fastest-growing Hispanic markets in the United States, and this dentist had seen the Hispanic population growing rapidly in the area near his office. He knew there were Hispanic families moving to the area that would need a good dentist. When his dental hygienist resigned to become a stay-at-home mom, he used the opportunity to hire a new assistant who spoke both Spanish and English. This made him operationally ready to market to Spanish-speaking potential patients. He had ads created in Spanish and also had several of his brochures translated into Spanish. He put a sign on the door of his office that stated *"Hablamos español"* (We speak Spanish). Soon, his practice was growing with new Hispanic patients.

What he didn't plan for was some backlash from a few of his original patients. He told me that when one of his patients saw the sign on the door in Spanish and then saw the brochures in Spanish, they berated him for "catering to people who speak Spanish—why would you work to communicate with them in their language? They should be working to communicate with you in English!"

I asked him how he'd handled this feedback from his patients. He said that he simply told them, "I understand your point, but my practice is dedicated to making people as comfortable as possible when they go to the dentist. Most people hate going to the dentist, or at least have some anxiety over it. I can't even imagine how much worse their anxiety is when they can't communicate well with their dentist or hygienist. So if I can take away a little bit of that anxiety for them, just by letting them know that we have someone on staff who speaks Spanish, then that's what I want to do. Because I want people to *come to the dentist*—not *avoid* the dentist. If letting people know that we have Spanish-speaking capabilities here makes them more likely to see the dentist on a regular basis, that's what I'm going to do."

I then asked him what his patient said to that. He replied, "My patient said, "That makes sense. I hadn't thought of it that way.""

The dentist handled the situation beautifully. He was polite but resolute, and he had solid reasons for his approach. By putting the comfort of the customer at the center of the conversation, he painted a compelling picture, and one that's pretty hard to argue with.

Here are the things you should do to help minimize negative feedback or backlash from your employees or core customers:

With Employees

- Review with all of them *why* you're going to target the new customer group. Most people are reasonable, and when a business opportunity is presented in facts and financial perspective, they will usually understand why the opportunity is important.
- Tell them exactly what you expect of them. Let them know their role and that you are interested in their feedback and suggestions for improving any processes along the way.
- Let them know that you are interested in hearing what customers say, whether it's positive or negative.
- Arm them with the statement that you want them to make. Your employees may find themselves responding to customers who express displeasure about your marketing to a new customer group, so tell your employees exactly how you want them to handle that and exactly what you want them to say. You and your staff need to speak with a unified voice.

With Customers

- Explain, as the dentist did, what your motivations are for reaching out to a new customer group.
- Do not apologize for your actions, but take the time to explain why what you're doing is a good idea.
- If your customer threatens to take his or her business elsewhere, politely state that you hope that doesn't happen, but that business is all about serving customers, and this is a new customer that you felt could be well served by your business.

Keep in mind that people are entitled to their opinions. However, they're not entitled to tell you how to run your business. If you know that reaching out to a new customer group is likely to build your business, ignore the naysayers and stay the course. The very fact that you're reading this book puts you far ahead of most people. Follow your instincts and follow the business opportunity. They will lead you to prosperity.

PART TWO ⟩⟩
Key Customers Who Could Drive Your Business Growth

CHAPTER EIGHT ▶
Different Ages Want Different Things

In Chapter 2, I gave a brief overview of key generational segments and how the manner in which they received information helped shape their consumer habits. In this chapter, let's dive a little deeper into these different generations with the idea that learning more about them may trigger ideas for you on new customer segment opportunities.

There are currently five core generational segments:

- The Matures (also called Traditionalists or Veterans, although in the latter case, the term refers to "veterans of life," not veterans of war)
- Baby Boomers
- Gen X (also known as Baby Busters)

- Gen Y (also known as the Millennials or Gen Next)
- Gen Z (also known as Gen Net)

Each generation has distinct characteristics and a "personality" of sorts. While not everyone from each generation fits the characteristics I'll outline here, there are broad generalizations that do apply. And for our purposes in this chapter, I will draw comparisons between the generations so that you can see how they differ in key ways.

MATURES: BORN BEFORE 1946

Convenience, Control, and "Like-Mindedness" Rule

The Matures are the oldest generation, those born before 1946. Their children are grown, and many of this generation have stopped working and have retired. They tend to have conservative views and are slower to adapt to technology, since many worked their whole careers without it (see Figure 8.1).

Crime and personal safety are some of their chief concerns, as well as financial stability. Matures often want the same products and services as any other consumer group, just in different sizes or

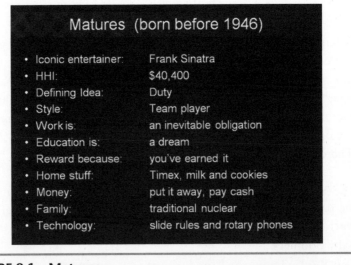

Matures (born before 1946)	
Iconic entertainer:	Frank Sinatra
HHI:	$40,400
Defining Idea:	Duty
Style:	Team player
Work is:	an inevitable obligation
Education is:	a dream
Reward because:	you've earned it
Home stuff:	Timex, milk and cookies
Money:	put it away, pay cash
Family:	traditional nuclear
Technology:	slide rules and rotary phones

FIGURE 8.1   Matures

quantities. This group also tends to really do their homework before buying something. They are careful about whom they do business with, and they want to know more about you before doing business with you. They're careful with their money and appreciate a deal. Therefore, if your company or product doesn't currently offer a senior discount, you may want to reconsider that. But make no mistake: just because Matures like a good deal doesn't mean they don't have money to spend. They have a solid financial foundation and strive to preserve their wealth while still enjoying the "fruits of their labor." The Mature generation also tends to be the most altruistic—they came of age when values such as "work is its own reward" and "the good of the group before the good of the individual" were pervasive. Therefore, products and services that have an altruistic angle (versus a selfish angle) will be more appealing to this group. A good example of this is recycling. When the push for recycling in local communities took place several years ago, Matures were the first to jump on board. Today, 81 percent of Matures recycle, compared to 74 percent of Boomers, 70 percent of Gen Y, and 80 percent of Gen X. Many Matures can remember when the idea of turning an old, unusable product into a new, usable one was just good sense. The practical aspect of recycling, as well as its altruistic appeal, made Matures the perfect "target" for recycling campaigns.

Also important for the Mature generation is *peace of mind*. Peace of mind can be expressed through a number of marketing messages. Some of the most effective include phrases such as:

- *Guaranteed* (as in "guaranteed repairs"). For mechanical repairs, terms such as *certified technicians* and *warranty* are compelling and effective. Remember, this group is cautious with their money and wants to make sure they are spending it wisely with a trusted company.
- *Safe and secure* (as in "keep your home safe and secure with XYZ's home monitoring service"). Personal safety is important to this group and many feel that their cities, neighborhoods, and homes are no longer safe.
- *Familiarity* (as in international travel). The Mature segment makes a very attractive target market for travel because they have both time and money. However, many Matures want to explore other

countries but don't necessarily want to hassle with language differences, differences in currency and customs, unfamiliar foods, and having to figure out on their own what to see and do. Some of the most successful travel tour groups have recognized this and have created special tours targeted to the Mature market. Beyond providing a great value for the money, the tour companies market themselves by touting their *familiarity* with local customs, the language, food, and the costs of goods and services. They emphasize that their guides are completely familiar with these countries, *so you don't have to be*. Their ads and brochures feature travelers eating a meal that the reader can recognize, in a setting that looks familiar and not strange, and perhaps chatting with others who look like the reader. And their ads feature a structured itinerary, so the traveler knows he does not have to figure it all out himself.

- *Everything you need* (as in "everything you need to start growing your own vegetables"). If you want to market effectively to Matures, one of the best tactics is to *ease their frustration*. One of the most frustrating aspects of buying something is realizing that you also have to buy something else just to get the first item to work. For example, let's say I want to wash and wax my car. I can buy the cleansing detergent and the wax, but if I've forgotten to buy (or didn't know I needed to buy) the chamois to dry the car and the Armor-All polish to make the tires look nice, I will become frustrated. However, if I found a "car wash kit" that contained "everything you need to wash and wax your vehicle," I'm likely to purchase that kit, even if the kit is more expensive than the items in the kit sold individually. I'm willing to pay for the peace of mind of knowing that I have everything I need to complete this project.

- *In control* (as in "in control of your health" and "in control of your finances"). Everyone likes to feel in control, but for Matures, this is an especially strong motivator. Matures have a lifetime of experiences, knowledge, and wisdom; they are information hungry; and they enjoy being well informed. Being well informed makes them feel in control of their lives and circumstances. If you were marketing a new financial service to Matures or marketing a new health service, you'd want to include a message about the benefit of being in control. A friend of mine lives in South Florida, where a significant percentage of the population is Matures. Years ago, she started a service to deliver groceries to older people who no longer could get out and drive as they used to. The business has been such a success that she's created another, compatible business, providing car service to Matures. Instead of just focusing on groceries delivered to a home, she identified that there are many Matures who want to get out and about but need someone to drive them. When she developed the service, she was smart about how she structured the pricing: she provided options, ranging from individual trips to discounts for multiple or set numbers of trips. By doing this, she not only fills a need in the market, she makes her customers feel in control, because they can choose the plan that best suits their needs.

- *Companionship* For many Matures, companionship is key. Without the hectic, busy lifestyle that goes with work and children, many Matures find themselves craving companionship and community. It's important to them that they stay connected. In marketing messages, stressing companionship can be a powerful selling point. Whether it's part of the benefits of joining a church, health club, or volunteer group, or whether it's part of the fun of travel or dining, companionship and socializing with others like themselves is important to Matures. Just *make sure that your product actually lives up to this promise*, though. In the case of my friend in Florida who developed the grocery home delivery service, she was an astute businesswoman who knew that homebound Matures would likely be lonely and craving human contact. Therefore, when she hired her delivery staff, she made sure they had the kinds of personalities and compassion that would make them well suited for the job. She knew that the drivers wouldn't just drop off the groceries and go; the customers were lonely and talkative and wanted to "visit" for a while with the driver. They were likely to ask the driver if they wanted a glass of iced tea, and they wanted to prolong the driver's stay. When she interviewed candidates for the delivery positions, she looked for sensitive, compassionate, patient people who wouldn't consider it an inconvenience to visit with an older person for 15 or 20 minutes when delivering groceries.

- *"Like-minded."* Many Matures want to live among and socialize with others who share their values and beliefs. This can be a powerful marketing message for Matures. It was used successfully by a retirement community called Independence Grove, a 180-acre, senior community in Hillsdale, Michigan. It's a community that is sponsored by conservative, local Hillsdale College. Hillsdale College has created a distinct model that can be described as "like-minded" retirement, or as the school's promotional material describes: "to extend the college's mission of educating for liberty." Free-market economics, patriotism, and conservative religious values are the bedrock of the community, and the residents who choose to make this their home tend to share similar values.

BABY BOOMERS: BORN 1946–1964

Retiring Baby Boomers—It's All About Them

The Baby Boomers get a lot of attention. As the largest population ever in the United States, with a corresponding population in Europe, Boomers have always defined every stage of their lives. When they were in their teens and 20s, Boomers wanted to change the world, and did so, with protests and marches that made the whole world stand up and take notice. As Boomers hit their 30s, Boomer women flocked to the workforce, rejecting the notion that a woman's only role was as homemaker and mother. As Boomers moved into their 40s and hit their peak earning years at work, they acquired material wealth as no generation before or since has (see Figure 8.2).

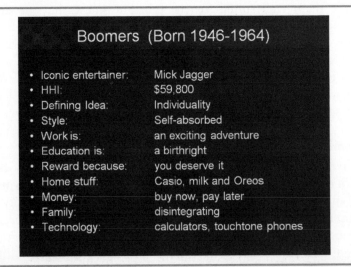

FIGURE 8.2 Baby Boomers

Boomers in Europe and North America are widely associated with affluence and privilege, as they became the wealthiest generation to date. In their 50s, Boomers focused on investments and making their money grow. They also focused on experiences: food experiences, travel experiences, sky-diving—you name it. Boomers tend to see themselves as perpetually young and perpetually fashionable. Everything they've ever done or needed is instantly in style, simply because of the size of their generation and their buying clout. For example, when I was growing up, the eyeglasses that my grandparents wore were pretty ugly. Typical glasses had thick lenses, sometimes as much as a half-inch thick, with the bifocal "half moon" prominent and visible. The frames themselves were clunky and ugly. But as the Boomers began aging and needed eyeglasses to read, "glasses" became "eyewear," and eyewear became fashionable. Today, gone are the thick lenses and hideous frames: the choices are numerous, and there are frames that fit every face and look terrific. And as for that bifocal "half moon"? Well, Boomers just won't tolerate it. After all, reading glasses are for "old people," and Boomers don't like to think of themselves as old. So they happily pay extra for the "invisible bifocals" with no discernable telltale marking of a "reading lens."

Boomers' vanity extends to all kinds of products: Botox and facial fillers, vitamins that promise youthful energy, Viagra and other intimacy-related products. The Boomers are going kicking and screaming into old age and there are hundreds of brands and products that are happy to milk this vanity for all it's worth. Boomers have never met a life stage they didn't want to redefine, and growing older will be no different. They are active and wealthy and, now, with the kids out of the house, they have more time on their hands than ever before. Boomers won't be retiring to sit on the porch and knit—they'll be windsurfing or going on safari. They want to try everything and do everything and leave their mark on the world. Consequently, these desires and demands are shaping everything from housing to leisure travel to financial services and health care to even the industry of dying. An economist that I recently heard at a conference stated the home of the future for Baby Boomers will be less than 1,600 square feet, highly energy-efficient, and have zero upkeep on the exterior: no lawn, no garden, nothing to maintain. Why? Because Boomers do not want to spend their time caring for lawns and gardens when they could be out playing. Adventure travel is already a booming (no pun intended) category, as Boomers crave "experiences," not just trips. Whether it's swimming with dolphins, biking through Italy, or climbing in the Alps, Boomers want to try it all. And not only do they have the money for the trip, they have the money for all the top-of-the-line gear for the journey and the personal trainer who will get them in shape to climb the mountain or bike through the countryside. Financial services are eagerly targeting the Boomers, too: for Boomers who worry that they saved too little or too late to continue to fund their lifestyle, there are financial products now like "longevity insurance," a fixed deferred-income annuity to help insure seniors against the biggest risk they will face in retirement: outliving their money. And when they do die, they can still be part of the fun: a company called Eternal Reefs offers a burial/cremation service where your ashes are mixed with concrete and turned into an artificial reef off the coast of Florida. As *Fast Company* magazine stated about this service, "Boomers will be scuba diving, even in the afterlife."

What do you need to know about marketing to Boomers? It's all about them. Make sure your message focuses on what's in it for them: convenience and appearance, sprinkled with a healthy serving of "you deserve it." And don't point out that they're getting older—Boomers don't see themselves that way, so creating a marketing message that states, "Feel (or look) young again," will backfire. Boomers already feel young and think they look pretty darn good. Boomers aren't looking for products and services to change their lives. They like their lives the way they are. They want products and services that will *complement* their lives and give them more choices. In the book *Advertising to Baby Boomers*, author Chuck Nyren points out that the way Boomers view amenities is different from previous generations. He uses the example of housing: homes in a planned community. He states that other generations look at homes and say, "Oh, it has this and this and this!" But Boomers see the same house and think, "This has great natural light for my plants and indoor garden" or "These hallways are nice and wide and I can lean my bike up and it won't be in the way" or "I can put up shelves in here for my books and CDs." In other words, they don't see a house loaded with amenities as a way of starting a new chapter in life. They see it as a way to complement *the life they already have*. They view products and services through the lens of "does this fit in with me, my life, and what I want to do?"

Because they look at products and services that way, there is no reason to be afraid of telling them everything they need to know about you and your product or service. Boomers don't have short attention spans. On the contrary, if something interests them, they'll read every word they can find on the subject. They'll do extensive research and comparisons, they'll educate themselves, and they'll compare notes with others. You don't have to "dumb it down" for Boomers; they're hungry for information, and if you can show how your product or service fits into their life, you can earn their business and loyalty.

Here are some key marketing platforms that resonate with Boomers and their values:

- *Quality.* Boomers have always wanted (and purchased), the best of everything. Whether it's gourmet food for their pets or special interest classes for their kids, high-end linens for their home, high-tech electronics or luxury vacations, Boomers want quality. They also know quality. They love to own the best and they know that the best lasts.
- *Choices.* While everyone likes to have choices, for Boomers, choices mean control. Having choices also communicates "freedom," and Boomers love to decide what they're going to do and how they're going to do it. For example, a travel tourism business that wants to attract Boomers would be smart to offer some tours that let the traveler choose how they want to spend their day. Unlike the Mature traveler, who may prefer to have a highly structured itinerary with a guide, a Boomer may want to choose from several different tour options, read extensively about each option, and then strike out on their own for the day.
- *Appeal to indulgence.* Boomers have worked hard and believe that they have "earned the right" to the things they want. Whether it's a new car, new shoes, gourmet ice cream, or an expensive face cream, Boomers feel that they "deserve" to pamper themselves. They enjoy their creature comforts and don't feel the need to save special things for "special occasions." They want to enjoy their special treats whenever they want. They like to indulge themselves and believe this is part of work/life balance. Whereas Matures often denied

themselves indulgences, and splurges seemed "excessive" and perhaps unmerited, Boomers feel just the opposite. Boomers feel entitled to splurge because not only can they afford it—*they earned it*.

GEN X: BORN 1965–1981

Authenticity is Everything

Generation X is a much smaller population than the generations that bracket them, the Baby Boomers and Gen Y. In fact, one phrase that aptly describes this is the "population hourglass," with Boomers and Gen Y representing the full top and bottom parts of the hourglass and Gen X representing the tiny "waist" of it (see Figure 8.3).

Gen Xer's are children of two working parents. And they are children of divorce: more than half of Gen Xer's parents divorced while they were growing up and living at home. This led to the term *latchkey kid,* referring to a child whose parent or parents worked and were not home when the child got out of school. Consequently, the child had a key to the house and was alone for several hours each weekday after school, before mom or dad (or both) came home from work. This time alone created children who were independent, responsible,

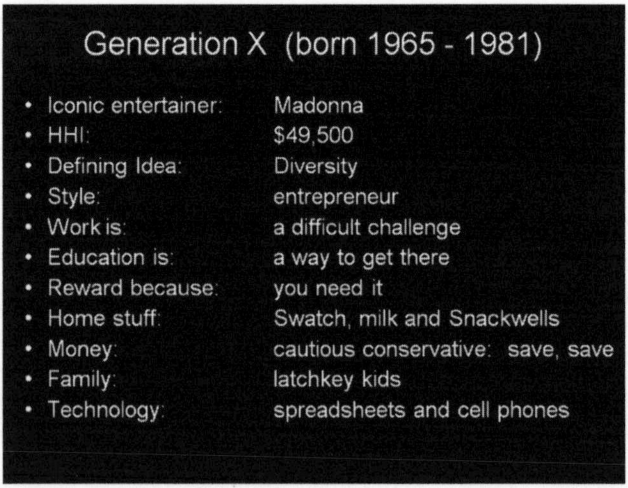

Generation X (born 1965 - 1981)	
• Iconic entertainer:	Madonna
• HHI:	$49,500
• Defining Idea:	Diversity
• Style:	entrepreneur
• Work is:	a difficult challenge
• Education is:	a way to get there
• Reward because:	you need it
• Home stuff:	Swatch, milk and Snackwells
• Money:	cautious conservative: save, save
• Family:	latchkey kids
• Technology:	spreadsheets and cell phones

FIGURE 8.3   Gen X

and self-reliant. They had to be; no one was there to help them with homework or snacks when they got home from school. They figured things out on their own. They are very resourceful and independent thinkers. They are resilient and adaptable. They're also very skeptical. Why? Because major institutions in their lives, such as marriage and workplace stability—things that should have lasted—*didn't*. They watched their parents divorce, often more than once. They also saw a number of large companies implode in the 1990s, and they, their parents, their friends, or loved ones were laid off for no reason other than corporate greed and dysfunction. They believe that the rug can be pulled out from under you at any moment; in fact, *they've seen it happen*, so the only person you can trust is yourself. Gen X also came of age when technology was really taking off. They love technology and see it as an integral part of their life. And speaking of life, they have active lives. This is the generation that coined the term *work/life balance*. They saw no need to sacrifice everything for the company because what does that get you? You may still be laid off. So their philosophy about work is that they'll give 100 percent when they're there, but when they're not at work, they're busy having a real life, and work better not intrude on that. Gen Xer's are self-oriented and pragmatic. They have an attitude of "survivalist." They believe that if they don't look after themselves, no one will, so they are committed to making their lives the best they can be. They're educated, and they're planners. Whereas the Boomers like spontaneity, Xers like having things mapped out for them. Their pragmatic viewpoint is drawn to logical equations: "If you do this, you'll get this." That's why investing and the stock market appeals to them; they understand that if you take these steps and invest in certain ways, you're likely to get a certain outcome.

Here are recommended approaches for marketing effectively to Gen X:

- *Develop products aimed right at them.* A great example of this is snowboards. Gen X sees downhill skiing as a sport for Baby Boomers. Boarding is for Gen X. Baby Boomers had Sony Walkmans; Gen X has iPods.
- *Use humor.* Gen X loves to laugh. They love smart humor and sarcasm, but also goofy messages, too. They see the humor and irony

and weirdness in everyday life, so why shouldn't marketing messages reflect the same?

- *Authenticity.* This is very a cynical generation, and they can spot the inauthentic very quickly. If your product or service is not high quality or does not deliver on its promise, you're history with this group. Make sure that what you say can be backed up with performance.

- *Avoid status marketing.* Because this generation is independent and values thinking for themselves, they are not as likely to have a "herd mentality" when it comes to following the latest fashion, fad, or status brand. In fact, many Gen Xers reject status brands precisely *because* others value them. Xers want to make their own statement. They want quality products that solve problems for them. Tell your story accurately and thoroughly and you'll impress them.

- *Stress value and consider pricing.* Because many Gen Xers grew up in single-parent households where money was tight, they tend to be more frugal than either Baby Boomers or Gen Y. They can afford a lot, but they choose to spend their money carefully. To appeal to Gen X, think carefully about your pricing and make sure that your product or service represents excellent value. Gen X has money, and they don't mind spending it; they just want to get the most for their money and feel that what they buy is a good investment.

GEN Y: BORN 1982–1994

Good, Fast, and Cheap Experiences

Gen Y is getting a lot of attention these days because they're fully into the workforce now, earning money and, therefore, able to make purchasing decisions like never before (see Figure 8.4).

This generation has some unique characteristics. Raised during the most child-centric time in history, this generation was showered with attention by their Baby Boomer parents. Parenting styles changed dramatically, from parent as "authority" to parent as "friend." This generation cares passionately about the Earth and their communities. They don't watch TV or read much, but they do listen to what their friends say. In fact, you can't tell them what to like or do—only they and their friends can do that. They love "experiences"—they want to experience things firsthand and then they will decide if they like it or not. They want real, authentic experiences and messages. They are

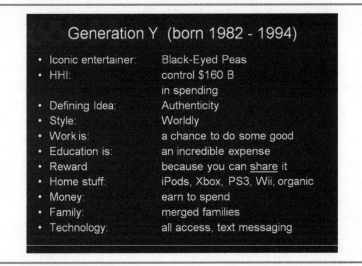

FIGURE 8.4   Gen Y

worldly because technology has been part of their lives, all of their lives. They don't know life without it. So how do you market effectively to Gen Y? Bea Fields, a Gen Y marketing expert, lists four key factors that Gen Y looks for in making purchase decisions:

- Cheap cost
- Good quality
- Fast service
- An "experience"

She cites Apple and the 99-cent music download as a perfect bull's-eye in targeting Gen Y. First, the cost was low. Everyone can afford 99 cents! Second, the quality is fantastic. Third, the transaction takes eight seconds or less. And last, music is definitely an experience.

Gen Y is more connected than any other generation has ever been. And not just connected to news and world events. Thanks to the Internet, they can learn about anything, at any time, 24 hours a day. No previous generation has ever had this ability *throughout their lives*. But in addition to staying connected to news and happenings, they are connected to their friends and world communities. They know people all over the world and form communities based on mutual interests and concerns. Their social networks mean everything to them. Even their dating habits are affected by this: Gen Y is more likely to date and socialize in groups rather than pair off as couples. But because they are so connected—information is everywhere and anyone can reach them—they are very selective about whom they listen to. And who they listen to are their friends.

If your product or service is going to succeed with Gen Y, you've got to be endorsed by their network of friends. And you'll do this by not overtly "pitching" them. This generation is not just wary of pitches—they flat-out reject them. Their mind-set is: "Don't just *tell* me why I should like your product or service; *show* me (and my friends). Let me experience your product or service for myself. If I like it, I'll tell everyone I know."

How do you show your product or service? You go where they are and get involved in their lives. This can mean sampling or demonstrating a product at a concert, movie, or extreme sporting event. Red Bull was initially launched in clubs. It was the perfect place to do so— young people having a great time at the club wanted to stay up late and keep the party going all night, and Red Bull helped them do that. Red Bull sampled extensively at all the hottest clubs. It wasn't about advertising Red Bull—it was about *experiencing* it. Bea Fields even suggests tattoo parlors as a place to expose your product or service to Gen Y: nearly 40 percent of Gen Yers have at least one tattoo.

Social networking is a must for anyone trying to reach Gen Y. Your product or service or brand should have a social networking site, such as a Facebook or MySpace page. It's a great way to share relevant information, tips, and insights without overtly "pitching" your business. It's a way to start a conversation with your Gen Y target and find out what they want and how you can best meet their needs.

GEN Z: BORN 1995–2004

Digital Natives

Generation Z makes up 18 percent of the world's population. Although they're still very young, they have access to technology and many tools, such as mobile phones, iPods, and computers, and this technology shapes their life in many ways. They are truly the digital generation. They are growing up in a world of equality, and they believe that men and women are equal. Additionally, their world is more racially and ethnically diverse than any previous generation's. In fact, Katie Hollar, chief marketing officer at law firm Lathrop & Gage and one of the savviest marketing professionals I know, recently made the comment that the new "communication gap" has less to do with age, race, or ethnicity and everything to do with technology. Her observation was that Gen Z is more likely to feel disconnected from you because of technology gaps rather than because you're of a different race or age than they are.

For Gen Z, it's all about the computer. They are the digital natives. All of their communication takes place on the Internet, and they are not inclined to possess strong verbal communication skills. In their minds, they don't need them. Because they have never known a world without the Internet, they do not consider it to be the greatest tool for mankind. It's always been there for them, so they take it for granted. They also take speed and instant gratification for granted; everything they want or want to know can be had instantly. Consequently, they are impatient and desire instant results. Gen Z also does not believe that you have to personally meet or know your friends. They can develop relationships over the Internet, especially through social networking sites. They form large communities online and can collaborate with hundreds of others online without ever knowing anyone personally.

So what does Gen Z want and expect? Here are a few insights that will help you in marketing to Gen Z, now and in the future:

- Online shopping and downloading.
- Speed and solution marketing that provides instant answers and fast purchasing.
- The ability to click and choose online, pay immediately, and receive an instant response so they can move on to something else.
- The ability to receive service from you without forcing them to the phone or suggesting they drop into your store.
- Environmentally friendly companies and products. Gen Z is expected to be the most environmentally aware generation to date.
- Electronic communication. Since they've grown up with mobile phones, and they spend their time texting and socializing online,

they expect their family, friends, and businesses to communicate with them electronically. In marketing to Gen Z customers, use such tactics as automated reminders, extended customer care using e-mail and text messaging, and prompting customers with personal messages.

- Humor. Habbo Australia, a social networking site aimed at teenagers and 'tweens (those between the ages of 8 and 12) in their Next Generation Survey, found that when asked, "What kinds of advertising do you prefer?," 46 percent of Gen Z said, "Ads that make me laugh."

- Mobile messaging. With Gen Z, you have to be ready to go mobile, and go mobile now. Smartphones can work with Web pages that are optimized for mobile devices. Work with a mobile marketing company to pilot a program and test messages and offers. As mentioned in Chapter 6, a company I recommend is LSN Mobile (www.lsnmobile.com). They are affordable and can work with any size project and any budget.

It's very likely you can sell your product or service to more than just one generation of customers. To market to different generations, you simply need to tap into the unique values and create messaging that resonates with what each generation cares about. Each generation has distinct characteristics.

CHAPTER NINE ➤➤
Women

Singles, Heads of Household, Working Moms and Stay-at-Home Moms, Home-Schooling, and More

Women comprise about half the population in the world. And women make up about half of the workforce in many countries. Yet it's said that women make 80 percent of the buying decisions in all homes. 80 percent! Combine that decision-making power with earning power, and you have an absolutely irresistible target consumer. It's no wonder so many companies are waking up to the fact that women can make or break their sales and even their brands.

But reaching women is not easy. Women—all over the world—are busy. Really busy! They juggle a lot: homes, children, marriages, jobs, cooking, cleaning, and more. Although in many households, men help out and chores and responsibilities are shared, in many other homes, women carry a heavier load of responsibilities than men. Women are busy and stretched thin. One article I read recently put it this way: the female consumer has a complex "web of duties" that makes her less than readily available.

But it's worth it to try to reach her. The female consumer has become the "chief purchasing agent" in today's household, and she can be a very, very loyal customer. That's why companies, from retailers like Home Depot and Target to financial investment firms like Citibank and Merrill Lynch to electronics retailers like Best Buy, are taking targeted approaches to marketing to women. It's good for business.

Now, obviously, women are not "one size fits all." There is no one "right" way to market to women, but there are many wrong ways. If you want to reach women consumers effectively, the first thing you'll want to do is *narrowcast* and define what kind of woman you want or need to reach. For example, do you want to market your product or service to moms or women without children? How about single women or married women? Does your target female customer work? Is she a full-time homemaker? Does she home-school her children or send them to private school? These are just some of the ways that the broad category of "women" can be subsegmented into a narrower group that can be more easily targeted. Let me give you an example of marketing to women that I think is smart, innovative, and clearly filled a market need.

Prior to starting her company, Barbara's Way, Barbara Kavovit was a contractor and spent 15 years in the construction business. She knew women were capable of making their own home repairs and thought there was a market for products targeted to women to help them make their home repairs a little easier. She also recognized the need for tools designed for a woman's hand. Tools for men are too large for most women's hands. She created a line of tools and products ergonomically designed for women's smaller hands, and she went a step further: she also created complete "how-to kits" so that women could do their own home repairs and have everything they need to complete a repair job. The company offers a complete leaky faucet repair kit, toilet repair kit, drain cleaning kit, and more. Of course, women can fix things around the house—it's just that many don't know the proper steps, nor do they have the tools they need and specific "how to" instructions. Barbara's Way products, such as the complete repair kits, not only offer the "stuff" a woman needs to make a repair, it empowers that woman with information; each kit comes complete with a step-by-step instruction manual, as well as "how to videos" on the company's web site. It's great to be able to watch a video of a woman making a household repair and showing that it's not that complicated, especially if you have the right tools.

This leads me to discuss the old adage "pink it or shrink it." When women were first recognized by companies as valuable consumers, the marketing philosophy often consisted of a "pink it or shrink it" strategy. Companies felt that all they had to do to a product to make it appeal to women was either make it pink (literally) or make it smaller. In the case of certain things like tools designed for the hand, "shrink it" is a viable, legitimate tactic. Women's hands usually *are* smaller than men's. That's not a stereotype—that's a fact. And with a product like a *hand tool*, it's perfectly acceptable to adjust the size of the product to reach a new customer segment.

But "pink it"? C'mon! Sure, women like color, but that doesn't mean the only color we relate to is *pink!* In fact, Barbara's Way products are mostly manufactured in a nice, medium blue. So who are the female customers that Barbara's Way products are targeted to? The company is clearly targeting single women, women who are interested in home projects and home repair, and those who are perhaps the head of their households. These are women who are likely to do more than one simple repair—they want *their own sets of tools*, which suggest that they make repairs or undertake projects on a regular basis. The web site for the company reflects that they know this about their target customer: the site is filled with helpful tips, typical home projects, Barbara's Blog, suggested improvements for the home, and money-saving tips. None of it is patronizing or condescending. In fact, it's all very empowering. When you see all the things that "Barbara" can show you how to do around the house, you get excited about the possibilities and you start thinking of the projects you want to tackle in your own home. Barbara's Way is doing it right: their products look good and fill a need, and their site is written with the female do-it-yourselfer in mind. I was particularly struck by a sentence on the site that referenced how much money could be saved by repairing your own toilet. It stated that you can save about $150 by making a toilet repair yourself. It went on to say, "Use the savings for a special dinner, a night at the movies, or anything you want." In my opinion, this is excellent advertising copy, clearly targeted to women. Men don't typically think of $150 savings in terms of a dinner out or a night at the movies with friends. But women do. In small, subtle ways, everything about the company, the brand and their product offerings reflect that they understand the female "do-it-yourselfer."

Another example of narrowcasting and marketing to a segment of the women's market is marketing to moms. While not all moms are the same, of course, there are some core values that cross racial, ethic, socioeconomic, and generational lines as well as geography. Maria Bailey, president of BSM Media, a marketing firm that specializes in marketing to mothers around the world, states that *moms around the world* share five core values:

1. Child enrichment
2. Health and safety of her family
3. Value
4. Time management
5. Simplifying life

These core values make sense. Regardless of what country you live in or what language you speak or how much money your family earns, if you're a mom, chances are, you agree with the list above. What mom doesn't want to enrich her child's life and experiences? What mom doesn't care about the health and well-being of her family? Many moms are in charge of the family budget, so making sure your product or service is seen as a solid value is critical. And moms are super-busy, so anything that saves them time or simplifies their life is viewed favorably. But because moms *are* so busy, they often see ads as too "intrusive" and something they "just don't have time for."

So how do moms get the information they need about products and services? From each other. In fact, research shows that what mothers value most is "hearing opinions from other moms." Therefore, if you want to reach moms, you need to use other moms to do so. A great example of this is how Fisher-Price launched a cradle and swing targeted to moms with infants aged 3 weeks to 12 weeks. Fisher-Price first identified women who shared two interesting traits: they were new moms and they were also bloggers. Fisher-Price then narrowed the list even further to those moms whose blogs received at least 2,000 unique visitors a week. There were 15 that fit that criterion. Fisher-Price gave those 15 moms a swing to use at home. The blogging moms gave feedback on the swing to a Fisher-Price product designer at a virtual play lab session. Sixty percent of the moms posted positive reviews of the cradle and swing on their blogs, thus spreading the word about the product and providing "testimonials" that other moms read. Some moms even included video of their baby in the swing. What a great way to reach moms—through a trusted source: other moms.

Narrowcasting and defining your female target is the first step to effectively marketing to women. The next step is to craft a message that will resonate with your target audience. While every woman's opinions are her own and women can't be lumped together into one group that shares a common viewpoint on everything, in my experience, I have found that women do tend to like and dislike certain things when it comes to the advertising and marketing that they see.

Here are key aspects that women really like or find appealing to them in marketing messages:

- *Authenticity*. In a focus group of women that my company recently conducted, the word *real* kept coming up over and over again. Women were asked to look at ads and discuss those they liked and didn't like, and why. The ads were different, and they were viewed by different women, of different ages and races, and from all different walks of life; yet time and again, they echoed that they want a marketing message to be "real." They shunned the overly airbrushed models and their perfect bodies in perfect swimsuits. They responded well to an ad showing a mom blowing bubbles with her child. Why? Because blowing bubbles with your child is relatable for most women. It's simple. And special. Keep your message real. Don't promise women the moon. Tell them what they need to know and showcase real life.
- *"Tools for our lives."* This quote came straight from a woman in a focus group, and I couldn't phrase it any better than this. "What we

want are tools for our lives," said a busy woman who owns a business. "We want solutions." Show a woman how your product or service can help her. Perhaps it will save her time. Perhaps it will make her life easier. Perhaps it will make her morning routine go more smoothly. Or it will save her money. Or her family will love it. There are a million things that women want help with. Figure out how your product or service is a "tool for a woman's life" and you're on your way. Olay products understand this. They created their Total Effects line in response to women complaining that they want a simple, effective skin care regime. Most women don't want to have to go through a complex, multistep process for their skin care. They want as few products as possible and they want them to really work. Olay created Total Effects to be a moisturizer, sunscreen, exfoliator, toner, and more, all in one product.

• *Show possibilities.* An ad for the iPad has no advertising copy at all. It simply shows a faceless woman with an iPad in her lap, her legs propped up, reading (see Figure 9.1). Her posture clearly communicates that she's relaxed. The ad shows that it's possible to see yourself in this image, to see yourself as relaxed and taking some time to read. A similar ad, from Birkenstock, shows the legs and feet of a faceless woman, in the same position (see Figure 9.2). The scene is a beautiful beach paradise. The woman's feet are perfectly pedicured, and she's wearing a pair of Birkenstock sandals. The only advertising copy states, "Color me comfortable." It shows us that we can relax and have quiet, tranquil moments and that part of the relaxation is being completely comfortable, even with what we wear on our feet. I find it interesting that these two ads use identical poses to appeal to women: relaxing with feet propped up. To me, that pose strikes a chord for most women: we don't get much time to relax and we dream of having a few moments here and there to do so. These ads show us what's possible within our lives (a moment of relaxation) and how their products fit into that moment. That's what makes them so effective—they are relevant to women.

• *Reflect aspiration, but in a realistic way.* Women aspire to many things, but want realistic, achievable, attainable imagery to identify with. So many ads try to reach women by showing images most women can't possibly achieve or even relate to: ads that feature teenage girls with perfect bodies selling cellulite cream, or swimsuit ads that showcase emaciated-looking models, or jewelry ads that

FIGURE 9.1   iPad Advertisement

feature gorgeous women dripping in diamonds. While most women want to look beautiful and have an appreciation for beautiful things, we also know what we actually look like and that we are not supermodels. Which is why an ad for clothing store White House Black Market is so effective. The ad simply features the

FIGURE 9.2   Birkenstock Advertisement

words *feel beautiful* in a gorgeous script. There aren't even pictures of clothes, although that's what the store sells. What they're selling in the ad is the feeling that new clothes give every woman. We feel beautiful when we're wearing something new and stylish. It's a great feeling. White House Black Market has totally tapped into why women shop. Their ad doesn't say, "Be sexier!" or "Look thinner!" It simply says, "Feel beautiful," and that's exactly how women feel when they buy new clothing.

- *Reflect values.* Many ads targeted to women are aimed at the superficial: the toothpaste that will make your smile brighter, the lipstick or perfume that will attract a mate, the jeans that show off your figure and smooth your tummy. Women say that what really resonates with them is when an ad or company reflects their values. And most women's values are far from superficial. Take Keds, for example. A print ad for Keds that tested very well among women of all ages shows a young woman, casually dressed (wearing Keds, of course), in a diverse group of friends (see Figure 9.3). The friends are of different races and ethnicities. The copy reads: "All Together Now." What the women in the focus group liked so much about this ad was that it showcased

FIGURE 9.3   Keds Advertisement

friendship, being casual, and spending time together as "what matters," rather than fashion. When you can tap into what someone values, in this case, *relationships*, you have a powerful grip on someone's heart and, ultimately, their wallet.

Here are some values that resonate with women in different life stages and with different pressures:

Moms. What's best for her family, security, doing all that she can to ensure the well-being of herself and her family.

Single women, no children. Empowerment, respect, being "recognized" (one woman said that single, childless women were overlooked by advertisers. She stated, "They make us feel invisible.") Satisfied with their lives ("We don't need to be part of a couple to be happy," said one participant).

Single women, head of household, with children. Success at single parenting, empathy for all that I'm juggling, solutions that will make a difference in my life or my family's life, planning for the future, feeling strong and successful because I'm independent.

Working women (both moms and childless). Solutions that give me more time for myself, information that helps me make good purchasing decisions, empathy for my demanding schedule and the fact that when I am at home, there is still work to be done.

Stay-at-home moms. Family first, nothing but the best for my children, child-centric and family-centric messages.

Home-schoolers. Protecting family values, conservative values, security of controlling content for your children and keeping them from harmful influences that contradict family values, like-mindedness.

What do women *not* want in marketing messages? Here's a list of things that many women find offensive, insulting, patronizing, or useless in marketing to women:

- "Anything that degrades us." Overt sexuality, skimpy clothing, showing women as sexual objects.
- Making light of infidelity. Many ads targeted to men seem to give a "wink, wink, nudge, nudge" on infidelity, implying that it's either OK or that all men would do it if they could get away with it. Most women find this insulting.
- Showcasing women as unintelligent, helpless, or nags.
- Showcasing women in traditional sex roles. "Why is the guy never doing laundry? Why is it always the woman using detergent?" asked one focus group participant.

To sum it up, women are not "one size fits all," and the best approach is to target your message to the values that will resonate with a woman's life and her priorities. Here is a list of do's and don'ts when developing marketing messages to women.

Do portray women as:	Don't portray women as:
Feminine	Helpless
Sexy	Slutty
Empowered	Aggressive
Sensitive	Whiny
Opinionated	Bitchy
Nurturing	"Your Mommy"
Emotional	Weak
Collaborative	Indecisive
Hip	Inappropriate
Smart	Cold, unfeeling

Remember, women make 80 percent of the purchasing decisions. Women are an important part of your loyal customer base. Appeal to their values, respect their thinking, and provide them with relevant information, and you will see your sales and profits soar.

CHAPTER TEN ➤➤
Immigrants

It's About Acculturation, Not Assimilation

All over the world, people are moving. Every day, immigrants arrive in every country and begin to establish their lives there. There are many reasons why people move: for educational opportunities, for love, for family reunification, and for economic reasons, just to name a few. And it's easier than ever for people to move because of the convenience and low cost of travel. Now, more than ever, it's possible for many people to live wherever they choose to in the world, and people relocate in numbers that previous generations never did.

Whether they stay for a few months, a few years, or for the rest of their lives, immigrants are an important part of every country's economy. New arrivals to a country buy goods and services. And if you treat immigrants as welcome customers to your business, most of the time you will be rewarded with loyal customers who will bring you even more business through referrals. Imagine yourself moving to a foreign country and really not knowing your way around, where to shop and do business, even basic things like where to get your hair cut or where to do your grocery shopping. What would you do? How would you begin to figure it all out?

One of the first things you might do is find out the communities where your fellow countrymen live. In almost every city and country, there are communities of immigrants who live in close proximity to one another. When you think about it, it's quite logical: as you adapt to a new home, you'd initially want to live around others like yourself, people who speak your language, and understand your native culture. These people would be able to "show you the ropes," how to adjust to your new life in this new city or country, because they'd immigrated there before you and have experience with the process. They would be able to advise you on what to do or not do and mistakes to avoid. They'd be able to point you to the grocery stores that carry the ethnic foods of your country or region, so that you could cook and prepare the food you like and are familiar with. They'd be able to direct you to businesses and people whom they found to be helpful and with whom they feel comfortable. And they would tell you to avoid places where someone had been rude to them, overcharged them, didn't provide good service, or even simply someplace where they'd felt unwelcome.

As a new arrival to a new city, area, or country, you'd listen to their advice and probably follow their recommendations closely. It would save you a lot of time and hassle. You wouldn't have to figure everything out on your own—you'd have others guiding you who had experienced it all before. This is why, all across the world, humans gravitate toward others like themselves, particularly when they find themselves in a new and unfamiliar place.

So how does this phenomenon affect you and your business? If your business is located in a place where there is a large or growing immigrant population, you can prosper greatly by serving these customers. Your business can grow immediately by making sales to immigrants, and if they are happy and satisfied with your product or service, they will almost certainly refer you to others who will do more business with you. This can be an enormously effective way to grow your business because referrals cost you nothing. You don't have to spend money on advertising or marketing; you simply need to do a great job taking care of each and every customer. Attracting immigrant groups to your business is a smart strategy, but it's important that you know that not all immigrants are the same. There is a process that each immigrant goes through called *acculturation,* and because it is a process, not all people will be in the same phase of the process at the same time. In other words, immigrants are not "one size fits all." Let me explain.

ACCULTURATION, NOT ASSIMILATION: TARGETING IMMIGRANT GROUPS BY ACCULTURATION

Every immigrant who arrives in a new country goes through this process called acculturation.

It doesn't matter if you are Polish and you move to Switzerland, if you are American and move to Greece, or if you're British and you move to India. Regardless of who you are and where you're from, if you move to another country, you will experience acculturation.

Many people use the word *acculturation* interchangeably with *assimilation,* but they really shouldn't. The two words mean very different things. Assimilation means you *forfeit your culture and adopt the habits and traditions of a new culture.* Acculturation means that you forfeit nothing. With acculturation, there are certain things you like and want from a new culture, but there are certain things that you want to maintain and retain from your primary culture, too. Think of it this way: assimilation is about "either/or" (e.g., I'm either Hungarian *or* I'm British"), whereas acculturation is about "and" (I'm Hungarian *and* I'm also British).

Acculturation is the merging of two cultures in close contact. It's what happens when a person moves to a new country or is exposed to a country's culture, values, and lifestyles. An example of acculturation is exemplified by one of my employees and her younger sister. My employee and her family are originally from Mexico City. Her younger sister is 7 and grew up in the United States. Although her younger sister was born in Mexico, she was very young when the family moved to the United States and, consequently, she really doesn't remember much about living in Mexico.

In Mexico, Christmas traditions are quite a bit different than they are in the United States. For one thing, "Santa Claus" does not play a role. Santa Claus is a European, and now, American folklore tradition, but Santa Claus is not a Latin American tradition. Children in Latin America do not wait for Santa to come down the chimney on Christmas Eve and bring toys to all the good girls and boys of the world. Rather, toys and gifts are brought to children on Three Kings Day, which is January 6.

But imagine growing up as a child in the United States and not being exposed to Santa Claus! It would be nearly impossible—Santa is *everywhere* in December: he's at the mall, he's on every TV commercial, every greeting card, and he's sung about in many Christmas carols. He's very much a part of the American traditions and the holiday season. My employee's little sister, having grown up in the United States, believes in Santa Claus. On Christmas Eve, her family prepares Mexican tamales to eat (traditional Christmas food in Mexico) and she waits eagerly for Santa to come down her chimney with gifts. But there's no way that her family is going to skip the Three Kings Day on January 6. Since Three Kings Day is an important holiday for them, they celebrate this day with gifts and they bake the traditional *rosca* (sweet pastry bread with a tiny doll baked inside to represent the Baby Jesus). Whoever gets the piece of *rosca* with the doll must throw a party on February 2, offering tamales and *atole*, a traditional Mexican drink, to guests. This little girl gets the best of both worlds! My employee's little sister receives gifts from both Santa Claus *and* the Three Kings. She and her family participate in *both* customs, not one or the other. This is what is meant by acculturation.

Now that we've defined acculturation, let's explore the varying degrees of it and how it affects consumers. There are four distinct mind-sets that reflect the differing levels of acculturation among immigrants.

The first is the *Cultural Loyalist*. The Cultural Loyalist is foreign-born, a recent arrival who has typically been in their new country for less than 5 years, and certainly less than 10 years. Because it takes a long time to learn a new language, these people are dependent on their native language to communicate, and they will consume mostly native-language media and marketing messages. They will often live and work among other immigrants from their homeland, and they tend to hold on to the traditional values of their native country. While these individuals may spend the rest of their life living in their new, adopted country, many dream of going back "home." In focus groups with Cultural Loyalists, we'll often hear comments like, "I am here working, trying to save up enough money to buy a little house back home." This is why these individuals are called Cultural Loyalists; while they live in one country, their heart and their dreams are "back home." They are loyal to their primary culture. They do not consider their adopted home to be their true "home" but, rather, a place to live and work "for the time being."

The second level of acculturation is the *Cultural Embracer*. The Cultural Embracer is also foreign-born, but these individuals have chosen to make their new country their permanent home. These people have left their country knowing that they are not "going back." They may have immigrated for educational, professional, or occupational opportunities or because they are married to or in love with a citizen of another country, and so on. Because they have adopted another country as their new home, they do not have a "visitor" mentality. They are eagerly embracing new foods, new music, and new traditions and are making new friends. That's why they are called *Embracers*—they embrace everything about their new, adopted home. These people tend to be slightly more educated and very aspirational. And while they may be bilingual or multilingual, they prefer their native tongue. How could they not? As foreign-born individuals, their native tongue will always be their first language, and consequently, it will almost always be easier for them to express themselves in that language.

The third mind-set and level of acculturation is the *Cross-Culturer*. The Cross-Culturer is the first generation to be born in the adopted country. Their parents are foreign-born. The Cross-Culturer is bilingual, having usually learned the family's native language first, at home, and the language of the new country next, at school. Because mom and dad (and often grandma and grandpa) are all foreign-born, the family communicates primarily in the native language and holds many traditions from their original country dear. The result is that Cross-Culturers are not only bilingual, but also *bicultural*, equally comfortable in the culture of the old country and the new. They easily live and work in two languages. While they may be verbally fluent in the language of their parents' country, this does not mean that they know how to read and write that language well. This is because their education and focus in school was on learning to read and write in the language of the country they were born in. Therefore, while they may be able to converse in their family's native tongue, it doesn't necessarily mean that they know the proper grammar or punctuation—where all the accent marks go and the rules of accents, for example. This is important to note: we often have clients with someone on their staff who falls into this acculturation category and who speaks another language, and the client expects that individual to help write or translate a brochure into that language. This individual may not be qualified to do that, based on their formal education and training in reading and writing. Cross-Culturers sees themselves as members of both cultures (the culture of their family's background and the culture of the country they were born in). They are very much in touch with their roots and their heritage.

The last level of acculturation is the *Cultural Integrator*. This is the fully acculturated individual. Although they were born in one country, they trace their roots and ancestry to another country. These people may not speak the language of their ancestry, or perhaps they do not speak it well. Cultural Integrators are usually more dependent on the language of the country they were born in. However, they tend to be very proud of their foreign heritage, and consequently, they experience a form of "retro-acculturation." Because these individuals are already fully acculturated, their "acculturation process" has them returning to their roots and embracing their history and traditions. For example, several decades ago, it was not necessarily considered an advantage to be bilingual (English- and Spanish-speaking) in the United States. In fact, in some parts of the country, there was a stigma attached to speaking Spanish, especially in schools. Latinos of older generations tell of being sent home from school for speaking Spanish or having "the nuns slap the back of your hand with a ruler for speaking Spanish." So the little Hispanic boy growing up in this era might have pleaded with his mom, "Mommy, please don't call me José! Why can't you just call me Joey like all the other boys?" In those days, it was about "fitting in" and being "just like everybody else." Today, most people recognize what a huge professional advantage it is to be bilingual (or multilingual), and as the United States becomes

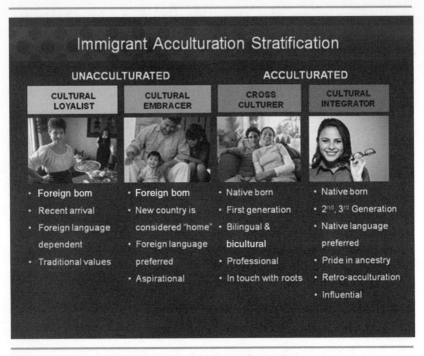

FIGURE 10.1   The Four Levels of Acculturation

more diverse, companies see the value of diverse cultures and celebrate different heritage and histories. Now, the same guy who begged
to be called "Joey" as a child proudly introduces himself as "José" as
an adult. That's retro-acculturation—the effort of reclaiming or getting back in touch with your cultural roots.

Figure 10.1 summarizes the four levels of acculturation.

As you can imagine, the way you'd market to a Cultural Loyalist
would be very different from how you'd market to a Cultural Integrator. Not just because of the difference in languages, but because
their needs would differ significantly. Let's take banking, for example. Suppose you're the marketing director of a bank and your community has a sizeable and growing Indian population. You know
that this represents opportunity for your bank, and you want to
create relevant marketing messages to entice potential Indian customers to your bank.

The first thing to do would be to identify the right products for
the right Indian profile. For example, because the Cultural Loyalist

is a recent arrival, chances are good that he will need basic financial services, such as a savings account and a checking account. He may also need and want money-wiring services, since it's very likely that he has loved ones in his home country to whom he's sending money each week. He may also need some financial literacy and education, since many from India have little or no experience in using financial institutions. It would not be practical to try to market mortgage products to this individual; as a recent arrival, he's not likely to have built up the credit history that will allow him to get approved for a mortgage yet.

For the Cultural Embracer, you could market not only your checking, savings, and money-wiring services, but also perhaps auto loans as well. Or mobile banking. For Cross-Culturers, there's probably no need to market money-wiring services at all, since their parents are with them in their new country. But this consumer makes an excellent mortgage prospect, as well as perhaps a prospect for a small business loan. And the Cultural Integrator can take advantage of all the bank's products and services, with the exception perhaps of money wiring.

Another example might be groceries. Everyone shops for groceries, but what Hispanics in the United States buy differs enormously, depending on levels of acculturation. The less acculturated, foreign-born Latino will tend to cook more with fresh foods and consume substantially more fresh fruit and produce than U.S.-born Latinos. Their snack choices lean toward salty snacks, spicy snacks, and cookies that are less sweet than most typical cookies made in the United States. More acculturated Latinos buy more packaged foods, prepared foods, and sweeter snacks. Additionally, the food choices themselves may differ: foreign-born Latinos will buy more mangos and avocados, more peppers, cilantro, and chiles—all ingredients used to make traditional Hispanic foods cooked from scratch. U.S.-born Latinos buy more cereal and pasta than foreign-born Latinos.

You can see how the acculturation model works—how you can segment your market opportunity for immigrants based not just on language, but on needs, traditions, and values. It's a useful tool in marketing to people who may not be like you. Every immigrant goes through this process. Some immigrants acculturate more quickly than others. Here are some of the factors (in no particular order) that affect the rate at which a person acculturates to a new culture or country:

- *Education.* For those who come to a new country with a solid education, chances are they are more prepared for what to expect and encounter. Typically, the higher the education level attained, the faster acculturation occurs.

- *Type of employment.* Those who work in lower-skilled occupations tend to acculturate at a slower rate than those who work in highly professional jobs. This is because highly professional jobs often require professional correspondence and strong communication skills in dealing with others. Together, out of necessity, these professional requirements accelerate the rate at which acculturation takes place.

- *Years of residency.* Typically, the longer a person lives in a new country, the more acculturated they become. Therefore, a recent arrival usually will not be as acculturated as an immigrant who has lived in that country for 20 years, for example.

- *Language proficiency.* Because language is a key part of any culture, the more proficient people become in the language of their new country, the faster they will acculturate. This is because the ability to speak the language means that greater understanding and comprehension will occur at all times. And understanding a new culture is the first step toward learning about that culture and adapting to it.

- *Willingness/ability to experience new things.* A significant part of learning about a new culture and adapting to it is the ability to experience aspects of that culture firsthand. Whether it's trying new foods, making new friends, listening to new music, or observing and participating in new traditions, holidays, and customs, people vary in how comfortable they are in trying new things. Immigrants who choose to live only among others who speak their language, who work and socialize only with others of their same culture, who cook only traditional foods from their original country, and so on will acculturate at a much slower rate than those who force themselves out of their comfort zone and continually try new things. Years ago, I worked with a man from Colombia. He'd been in the United States for about four years at the time, and he had received his master's degree in the United States. Although he came to the United States knowing quite a bit of English, he really worked hard to hone his English-speaking skills. One of the things he did was take a job as a telephone switchboard operator at a company. He said it was the most challenging thing he'd ever done because he had difficulty understanding the callers, and they often had difficulty understanding him as well. But he forced himself to stay with the job because it really stretched him—it made him work on perfecting his English, and he learned rapidly how Americans *actually speak in day-to-day living*, which is very different from the textbook and classroom ways that language is taught and presented. He also was open to trying anything and everything that was new to him. He once asked me to take him to a baseball game, and while we were there, he wanted a large, barbequed turkey leg. These turkey legs are enormous, and personally, I don't like them; they seem greasy and kind of revolting to me. I told him this and suggested a hot dog or nachos instead, but no, he wanted the turkey leg. Why? Because all the other men were walking around at the game eating the turkey legs, so he wanted to try one, too. That kind of openness and his willingness to try new things and put himself in situations that were tough or demanding really sped up the process of his acculturation.

In the next chapter, we'll do a deeper dive into a key immigrant group for North America—the growing U.S. Hispanic market.

CHAPTER ELEVEN ⟩⟩
Hispanics/Latinos: North America's Fastest-Growing Ethnic Minority

There is a large, national, wireless telecommunications company that you know. They're big, successful, and they're everywhere. Perhaps they are your carrier for your mobile phone—it's quite likely. I was at a marketing conference for the telecommunications industry, and I was the keynote speaker. My topic was the tremendous importance of the Hispanic population. For the telecommunications industry, this consumer group is huge, absolutely a goldmine, because not only are Hispanics the largest and fastest-growing ethnic minority in the United States, they also index higher in the purchase and use of mobile communications devices than any other race or ethnicity. The Hispanic population is a "perfect storm of opportunity," and everyone at this conference wanted to learn more about how to market effectively to this market segment.

After my presentation, several people came up to me to chat and ask questions. One woman introduced herself as a marketing executive for this large, national wireless company.

She stated that she enjoyed my presentation and that no one in her company needed to be convinced of the value of the Hispanic consumer market. She said, "What we struggle with is how to reach this customer. We know how important they are—we just don't know how to market to them. In fact, we made a huge effort a couple of years ago to reach Hispanics and it was a big flop, so we know we did something wrong. We just don't know what."

I asked what their marketing effort consisted of and she replied, "We did a huge Cinco de Mayo promotion in Miami, and it just failed miserably." I paused for a moment, looked her in the eye, and said, "Cinco de Mayo is a Mexican holiday. Miami is mostly Cuban. Maybe the Cubans don't give a flip about the Mexican holidays!"

CINCO DE MAYO IS *NOT* MEXICAN INDEPENDENCE DAY

That company made a classic mistake in thinking, "Here's a Hispanic holiday—let's build a promotion around that," not understanding that (1) the holiday must be relevant to the target audience, and (2) if you're going to build a promotion around a holiday, make sure it's a holiday people actually care about and celebrate. In this case, assuming that all Hispanics celebrate Cinco de Mayo was their first mistake. It would be like building a U.S. promotion around Canadian Boxing Day. Although English is spoken in both Canada and the United States, that doesn't mean the same holidays are observed or that Americans have any idea what Canadian Boxing Day is really about in the first place.

The second mistake was assuming that Cinco de Mayo is a big holiday at all. It's not, not even in Mexico. In Mexico, Cinco de Mayo is not widely celebrated. It's a day that commemorates the victory of the Mexicans over the French in the battle of Puebla. In the United States, Cinco de Mayo has become a "holiday" for partying, much like St. Patrick's Day is. The beer manufacturers created "holiday hype" around Cinco de Mayo (May 5th) because it fit well into the summer beer-drinking season and is several weeks ahead of Memorial Day.

Also, many Americans mistakenly believe that Cinco de Mayo is Mexican Independence Day. It's not.

You can see why the wireless company's promotional effort in Miami failed. And while you may be shaking your head or chuckling over the folly of this, you can also see why it is so important to not only understand *who* you're message is targeted to, but *what* that message really says in the first place.

Let's take a look at one of the most powerful and permanent population shifts happening in the world right now: the growing Hispanic population in the United States and North America.

WHY THE U.S. LATINO MARKET IS SUPER *CALIENTE*

Let's start with a little "Latino 101," a few facts to "set the table" so you can see how valuable this customer segment is today and just how valuable it will become in the next few years. But first things first: Latino or Hispanic? I wish I had a dollar for every time someone asked me which word is the "correct" word or the "right" or "politically correct" word to use. The answer is that both words are acceptable and most people use them interchangeably. While neither word is good or bad or right or wrong, it doesn't mean that people don't have individual preferences. For example, I prefer the word *Latino,* whereas most of my employees would probably describe themselves as Hispanic. They may be more comfortable with *Hispanic* because that's the word they were most familiar with when they were growing up. But here is the key difference between the words: "Latino" includes Brazilians, who are not of Spanish descent and do not speak Spanish (Brazilians speak Portuguese), but they are Latin American. And as Latin Americans, they subscribe to certain Latin characteristics: family values, food, faith, and cultural beliefs and traditions. If you call a Brazilian "Hispanic," he'll most likely correct you and he should. However, if you call him "Latino," it's usually quite acceptable.

Another key fact to know is that there is no such race as the "Hispanic race." Hispanic is an ethnicity, not a race. (The four races are White, Black, Asian, and Native American Indian or Alaskan Native).

There are several reasons why the Hispanic market is getting a lot of attention in the United States these days. It all comes down to what

I call "The 3 L's." The 3 L's stand for *large, lucrative,* and *loyal.* That's what every company, organization, and brand wants: a large enough group of people to sell their products and services to, a group that can afford those products and services, and a group that will keep coming back and do more business.

THE "SIZE OF THE PRIZE"

As of this writing, the U.S. Hispanic population is just over 50 million, comprising 17 percent of the total U.S. population. If you're like me, that's a staggering number to get my head around. Just how many is 50 million? Consider this: *there are more Latinos living in the United States than there are Canadians in Canada.* By 2020, *one in five* people in the United States will be Hispanic. One in five! No business or organization can afford to overlook one in five people. Additionally, Hispanics are now the largest and fastest-growing ethnic minority in the United States, eclipsing the African-American population in size and Asian population in rate of growth.

The influence of this exploding population is seen everywhere: in food, music and entertainment, sports, media, and politics. For example, look carefully at your grocery store; new products that cater to Latino tastes now fill shelves of supermarkets everywhere. Tortillas now outsell bagels two to one! Salsa is now the number one selling condiment in the United States. Lay's makes a *limón* (lime) potato chip. *Dulce de leche* (caramel) is everywhere: Betty Crocker offers *dulce de leche* frosting, it's one of Häagen Dazs' best-selling flavors of ice cream, and even M&M's has tested *dulce de leche* candies in select markets. And it's not just new flavors: American brand icons are even creating new *products* to capture Latino customers. In addition to pudding and gelatin, Jell-O now makes instant Jell-O flan (custard). Oreos, the best-selling cookie in the world, has created *dulce de leche* Oreos, the only one of its 44 varieties that is ethnically inspired.

None of these companies is making an effort to market to Hispanics out of a sense of "political correctness." They market to this group because the opportunity to grow sales and profits is enormous. That's because, in addition to the sheer size of this population and the rate at which it's growing, the segment also has tremendous buying power and is very brand loyal.

The average U.S. Hispanic household income is $52,725 (Claritas 2009). That's a solidly middle-class income with significant financial clout. Based on their income and the size of the population, Hispanics now have the greatest purchasing power of any racial or ethnic minority in the United States. And this customer segment also appreciates and responds to brands, products, and services that are high quality and provide them with great customer service. In fact, a study done by CNW Research showed that Hispanics, more than any other racial or ethnic group, tend to be more likely to stay with a product or service if they are satisfied.

So how can you capitalize on this large and lucrative and loyal market to grow your business? And how can you do so and avoid making cultural blunders or mistakes that may come across as insensitive? Here are the five essential steps to creating a great Hispanic marketing plan.

STEP 1: "LATINO-READY" AND "LATINO-FRIENDLY"— OPERATIONAL READINESS IS EVERYTHING

As you think about marketing to Hispanic customers, ask yourself this question first: *is your business prepared to serve the Hispanic customer?* By that, I mean that you must look at all aspects of your business through the "lens" of someone who is Hispanic (and likely speaks Spanish) and determine if it would be possible (or relatively painless) to do business with you. This is what I call *operational readiness,* and it is comprised of two key characteristics—being "Latino-ready" and being "Latino-friendly."

Latino-Ready

Being "Latino-ready" means that your business infrastructure can support doing business in Spanish. First and foremost, it means having someone on staff who can speak Spanish. This is the cornerstone of truly being able to attract the Hispanic consumer to your business and serve them effectively. If you market to Hispanics, they'll come. And when they do, many will need to, or want to, speak Spanish. If you don't have anyone who can assist a Hispanic customer in Spanish, you've essentially just driven them into a brick wall. Having

Spanish-speaking personnel, whether in a retail store or at a customer service call center, shows that you have prepared your business and are ready to serve the Spanish-speaking customer in their language of preference. When you have the opportunity to hire someone or add staff, advertise for and interview people who are bilingual. Schools and community colleges are great places to recruit because many schools have a growing Hispanic student body. Spanish media in most places also offer free job postings for employers, and the media outlet (radio station, newspaper, etc.) will usually also translate your ad posting at no charge. Catholic churches that hold Mass in Spanish and the Hispanic Chamber of Commerce are also great places to post ads. Be sure your ads spell out that you need "bilingual" skills, not just "Spanish-speaking." A client once advertised for Spanish-speaking sales associates and that's what she got: candidates who spoke Spanish but not English.

What if you're a small business owner and you have someone on your staff who speaks Spanish, but you have two locations and your bilingual employee can't be in two places at one time? In that case, you can develop a process that lets customers know that you're going to help them in Spanish, but that the "technique" may be a little un-conventional. As mentioned in Chapter 4, Mattress Firm, a national mattress retailer, developed a process that assisted both their customers and their employees. When a Spanish-speaking customer walked into a store where no one on staff spoke Spanish, an associate would smile, greet them, and hand them a card that was printed in Spanish and read: *"Hi! I don't speak Spanish, but I'm going to call someone at another of our locations who does. In the meantime, please fill out the back of this card so that we may serve you better."* The back of the card had a bilingual checklist that asked what the customer was look-ing for (twin, full, queen, or king-size mattress), whether they had any special needs or problems (back pain, neck pain, etc.), whether they preferred a soft or firm mattress, and so on. The customers loved the card. They loved that it was so professionally printed and well thought out. They loved that they were being helped in Spanish. And the sales associates loved it, too; the English-speaking employee could call a bilingual associate and let them know what the cus-tomer's needs were (e.g., they want a queen-size mattress, extra firm). Together, the team would help the customer and close the sale. Their process wasn't very sophisticated, but it was effective and it helped increase sales. It also improved employee morale because English-speaking associates now had a way to work with Hispanic customers that they'd never had before.

"Latino-ready" also can include things like having information, literature, or a web site in Spanish, having signage and policies in Spanish, and perhaps even having specific products that cater to Hispanic needs or tastes. Let me give you an example.

Laredo, Texas, is right on the border of Texas and Mexico. As such, 98 percent of the population of Laredo is Hispanic, and the local Walmart stores reflect the needs and consumer tastes of the market. Not only is virtually everyone who works at the stores bilingual, but all the signage in the stores is bilingual, and all policies, such as warranties, returns, and exchanges, are posted in Spanish as well as English. This makes it easy for their clientele to do business with Walmart. Their stores are "Latino-ready." Even their product offerings and selections cater to Hispanic needs and tastes. For example, a few years ago, the general manager of the one of the Walmarts in Laredo gave a fascinating interview on how he'd observed that Hispanic shoppers differ from non-Hispanic shoppers. He noted that brightly colored blouses sell better than neutrals. And he noted that women's jeans were not selling well at all. Why? Because Walmart's purchasing power comes from buying large quantities of products at low prices and distributing those products throughout all of their stores. The women's jeans that Walmart stocked at the time didn't flatter many Hispanic women's figures. You see, many Hispanic women have smaller waists and larger hips than non-Hispanic women. So the jeans that were in stock at the Walmart in Des Moines or Boise might sell well. But in Laredo, those same jeans gapped at the waist on the majority of Hispanic women shoppers and were too tight through the hips. This savvy store manager was somehow able to rectify this with his corporate buyers, and they changed their inventory mix to better suit the needs of Hispanic women. They started stocking jeans that were cut smaller in the waist and were more forgiving in the hips. And guess what? The jeans started flying off the shelves.

Another example of creating a product just for the Hispanic market is Minute Maid's *Limonada*. *Limonada* is limeade. In the United States, lemonade is far more common, but in Latin America, and particularly, Mexico, you won't find lemonade. You'll find *limonada*, because limes grow naturally and plentifully there and lemons don't. Limes are widely used in lots of food and drinks—limes are squeezed on fish and into beer and sangria—they're pretty much used all the time. So it makes sense that Minute Maid wouldn't just try to market orange juice or lemonade to Hispanic customers. They were smart and created a whole new product specifically for this consumer. And they went several steps further: the package itself is bilingual, but the Spanish is first. The package says "*Limonada* • Limeade" (see Figure 11.1). It was the first product packaging I ever saw in the United States where Spanish was *first* and English was second. But it makes complete sense for this particular product,

FIGURE 11.1   Minute Maid *Limonada*

because the primary target for *limonada* is Hispanics, and probably foreign-born Hispanics at that.

Even the Girl Scouts have expanded their cookie offerings with new, Hispanic-inspired flavors and varieties. From an earlier cookie version called *Olé Olé,* to *Dulce de Leche* today, the Girl Scouts' cookies that are created for the Hispanic market aren't just given clever Hispanic names. They're also created for Hispanic *palates*— the cookies are less sweet and sugary than most cookies you'd buy or find in a store in the United States. That's because American cookies are much, much sweeter than Mexican or Latin American cookies. For many Hispanics, American cookies are simply too sweet; they prefer cookies with less sugar and more subtle flavors, like vanilla and cinnamon. And, of course, the box features photos of Hispanic-looking girls (see Figure 11.2).

Being "Latino-ready" is very important. Before beginning any marketing to this customer group, make sure your business is as "ready" for this customer as it can be. At the end of this section, you'll find a checklist that will help you review key areas to examine in your business to ensure operational readiness.

FIGURE 11.2   Girl Scout Cookies

Latino-Friendly

Just as important as being "Latino-ready" is being "Latino-friendly" to effectively cultivate Hispanic customers. Some would say that of the two, being "Latino-friendly" is *more* important. That's because friendliness is universal and is always appreciated. You can travel the world over and not speak any language other than your own, and you will find yourself gravitating toward those people, businesses, restaurants, and places that are "friendly" and make you feel welcome.

Being "Latino-friendly" doesn't cost a thing. It means making sure your business is a place where Hispanic customers are going to feel welcome and appreciated. And just like the Latino-ready step, it starts with your staff. Even if no one on your staff speaks Spanish, they can be Latino-friendly. It's about eye contact, warmth, sincerity, helpfulness, and personal service. Essentially, it's all the basics of good customer service and good common sense, rolled into one. A store manager at Sherwin-Williams, the largest retail paint company in the world, told me that he didn't have anyone on staff who spoke Spanish at his store in Dallas, but he had a large and thriving clientele of Hispanic customers. I asked him how he served and handled his customers and he said, "We make sure they know that we want their business. We make them feel valued and welcome. When they walk in the door, we make eye contact, smile, and say, *'¡Hola!'* [*Hola* is Spanish for "hi"]. When they see us smiling and greeting them, they smile back and we start to help them. Sometimes there is a bit of a communication gap, but between our efforts and the customer's, we can always work it out. We know a few words in Spanish; they know a few words in English. They tend to shop as a family, so we have lollipops for the kids and coloring books for them, too. You see, mixing paint can take a while, so we want to make sure the kids don't get bored. And the parents really appreciate that. When they leave, we always say "Gracias!," and they always laugh and smile. They like coming to our store, and we know this because they bring others—the referral business is huge."

Comments like this are typical. Businesses such as that manager's are successful with Hispanic customers, not because they are

Latino-ready, but because they are Latino-friendly. There are reasons why your business may not be very Latino-ready: perhaps it's difficult to find bilingual staff, you have no control over products and services provided, and so on. But *there is no reason to not be Latino-friendly.* It will cover a multitude of shortcomings, and it positions you better in the customer's eyes than any amount of marketing you can do. It is possible to be Latino-friendly without being Latino-ready. And vice versa. But if you can be only one of those, be Latino-friendly. Let me tell you a story.

There is a large, national bank. You probably know them or have heard of them. They are everywhere in the United States. Several years ago, they got very serious about their Hispanic marketing efforts, and this bank is now very, very "Latino-ready." Everything you could want is available in Spanish: their web site, the ability to do online banking in Spanish, all their brochures, their point-of-sale materials in the bank are all bilingual; their call centers are staffed with bilingual operators and customer care professionals; and they offer highly competitive rates for money wiring—you get the picture. They are about as "Latino-ready" as a business can be.

One day, I was in the bank, waiting in line behind a Hispanic man. He had a check to cash and his U.S. passport for identification. He didn't have a driver's license. Perhaps he didn't have a car. After all, what do you need a driver's license for if you don't own a car or drive? And it seems obvious to me that a federally issued passport trumps a state-issued driver's license as a valid form of ID anyway. The man put his check and his passport down in front of the teller and said, "Please." It was pretty clear what he wanted: to either deposit or cash the check. The teller folded her arms across her chest, looked at him, and in a loud and snotty voice said, "Driver's license!" He shook his head, and held out his passport again, as if to say, "I don't have a license, but I have *this,*" but she was unmovable. She stood there, arms crossed, every bit of her body language implying that she knew exactly what he wanted, but she sure wasn't going to try to help or even meet him halfway. The customer stood there and said "please" again, and the teller raised her voice and yelled, loudly enough for everyone to hear, "No driver's license? No cash-o check-o!" The customer may not have spoken

English well, but he knew he was being insulted and mocked and, after what felt like an hour to me, but was probably just a few seconds, he left. That may be the end of his story, but my part continues. I was next in line. When I walked up to the same teller, she sweetly asked me how she could help me. Here's how our conversation went:

ME: "Just a second. I have a question—why didn't you cash that man's check?"

TELLER: "Well, he didn't have a driver's license."

ME: (pivoting, looking all around the bank): "Hmmmm . . . I don't see any signs stating that if you want to cash a check, you have to have a driver's license. That's your policy? I don't see that posted anywhere. In fact, I cash checks here all the time and no one ever asks me for my driver's license."

TELLER: "Well, those people shouldn't be here anyway."

Those people? *Those* people? People with U.S. passports? No, of course not. She meant Hispanics. It was outrageous. It was offensive. And it was wrong. But the point I need to make is this: that bank was Latino-ready all the way. But they were *not* Latino-friendly. It all came down to the actions and behavior of that one woman, the teller. She is the person the customer had the experience with; therefore, she *is* the bank to him. And all the effort that they put into being operationally ready, all the money they sunk into brochures, collateral materials, a web site in Spanish, and so on—all of it is wasted if that's what the customer's experience is like. In fact, the Latino-readiness of the bank made the situation even worse. Because when you've made your business Latino-ready and you are actively promoting your business to Hispanics, especially in Spanish, you're sending a message. That message is: "We want your business. Come to us. We're ready to help and we can serve you. In Spanish." To set the consumer's expectations in one way and then to deliver an experience that makes that same consumer feel unwelcome and unwanted is confusing, and frankly, they feel like they've been lied to. It's misleading. It's a complete waste of your time and money if you are Latino-ready, but not Latino-friendly.

Let me tell you another story. This one has a different outcome. This story is about an auction house in Indiana, one of the largest and most successful independent auction houses in the country, Christy's of Indiana. It's owned by a man named Jack Christy, who may be one of the nicest, kindest, and smartest people I've met. Jack and his company were selected for a special pilot program by the National Auctioneers Association (NAA). The NAA wanted to do an exploratory program to see if they could increase the number of Hispanics attending auctions, and they hired us to help them. Auction houses auction off all kinds of items, from property to automobiles to collector's items, household items—you name it. The NAA selected a few of their best auction owners to participate in this program, and that's how I met Jack.

Jack's auction house is located in Indianapolis. At the time of the pilot program, he did not have anyone on his staff who spoke Spanish. They weren't very "Latino-ready" at all. But Jack saw the business opportunity that Hispanic residents in the area represented, and he knew he could grow his business if he could get them to experience an auction at his facility. The first thing he did, though, was have a "kickoff" meeting with all of his employees to fill them in on the pilot program, what they were trying to accomplish, and the important role each and every one of them played in making these new customers "feel like they've come to the right place." Jack shared with them Hispanic population and growth numbers, so that they would understand why this program was important. He shared with them every element of what they'd be doing, so they were informed and "in the loop" and had a chance to ask questions. And he signed everyone up for lunchtime Spanish lessons with a local teacher who came to their facility weekly to teach basic Spanish phrases.

Well, the employees *loved* it. They all understood what was going on and why, what was expected of them, and they were excited to be part of a national "test" program. About a month after the kickoff meeting, my staff went to Indianapolis for a follow-up meeting with Jack and his team. I got a call from one of our associates there who excitedly told me, "Kelly, you won't believe it! As Jack was walking us to the conference room today, we noticed little brightly colored Post-It notes stuck on everything. On *everything*! On walls, on pictures, windows, on the refrigerator in their break room, even on the copier!"

I replied, "Post-It notes? What for? What do they say?" And my employee replied, "They have the Spanish word for that item on them! So the Post-It note on the window says *"ventana"* and the note on the light switch says *"luz."* It's so amazing, and Jack said it was the employees' idea! They're all so into it and they are trying so hard to be Latino-friendly." Jack later told me that, as their Hispanic clientele grew, their Spanish-speaking customers would smile about the notes and often helped with the proper word for an object. Several customers even asked for the English word to be added to the notes so that they, too, could pick up the words. Now *that* is Latino-friendly! Why would a Hispanic customer want to do business anywhere else?

That example shows how even the little things can make your business Latino-friendly. Don't be afraid to try. Put your heart into it and give it your best and warmest effort. You'll be rewarded. But just to get you started, here's a checklist of some things to consider as you think about preparing your business to serve Hispanic customers:

Latino-Ready

- Spanish-speaking staff (at least one individual to start, then others to make sure you have adequate coverage).
- Have bilingual associates record their voicemail greetings in Spanish and English.
- Telephone system options in Spanish.
- Information on your web site in Spanish, even if it's just one page of frequently asked questions (FAQs).
- Products that may be right for Hispanic needs and tastes.

Latino-Friendly

- Cultural sensitivity training for employees (e.g., *"Talking louder does not make someone bilingual"*—an actual customer comment from a Hispanic focus group).
- Customer service and customer care training—smiling, greeting customers in a welcoming, friendly manner.
- Accommodating families shopping and/or making decisions together (more chairs in a waiting room or office, small toys for kids).
- Being patient with questions—often, Spanish-speaking customers will have more questions about a product or service.

- Adjustment of hours, if necessary. An evening appointment may need to be 8:00 PM rather than 6 PM to accommodate a Hispanic customer's schedule. For example, many Hispanics work in the hospitality or construction or service businesses, where hours are long and not necessarily 9 AM to 5 PM. Therefore, if you're an insurance agent or a realtor and you want to meet with someone "after work" to sell them insurance or show them a home, be aware that it may not be possible for them to meet you at 6 PM. They may need to meet you considerably later than that. (We hear time and time again in focus groups that an "optimal evening appointment is 8 PM.")

Now that you have taken the most important step of making your business Latino-ready and Latino-friendly, it's time for Step Two: determining whether to use Spanish to reach your Hispanic customer target.

STEP 2: WHEN TO USE SPANISH IN MARKETING MESSAGES

To market effectively to Hispanics, it's very important to consider using Spanish. This is because, as of this writing, 61 percent of all Hispanic adults in the United States and more than 50 percent of all Hispanics in Canada are foreign-born. And while many foreign-born Hispanics may be bilingual, their first language will be Spanish. A frequent comment in focus groups among Hispanics is "I speak and understand English, but I prefer Spanish. I get more information about a product or service when it's advertised to me in Spanish." We've also frequently heard comments like: "Using Spanish creates an emotional bond with me. It tells me that you understand something about me and that you want my business."

Your marketing efforts may call for the use of Spanish to communicate effectively with your target prospect. Or not. It all depends on what you're selling and to whom. The majority of all Hispanics in the United States, adults and children, foreign-born and U.S.-born, say that they prefer Spanish, in any situation, business or socially. But when you break it down by age, acculturation, or even different situations, different snapshots emerge (see Figure 11.3).

Typically, U.S.-born Latinos under the age of 35 prefer English. But they may pepper their conversation with Spanish phrases or even

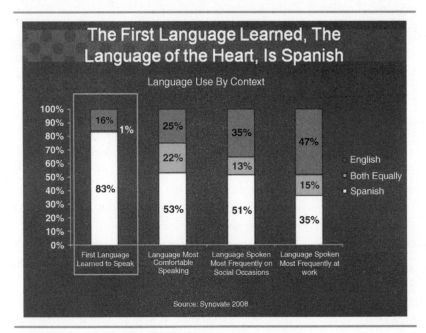

FIGURE 11.3   Hispanics' Language Use Varies
Source: Synovate's 2008 U.S. Diversity Markets Report

speak "Spanglish" at times. In some cases, a word in Spanish may fit better than an English word, and vice versa. For example, it's not uncommon for Hispanic youth who primarily speak English to greet each other in Spanish: *"¿Que pasa?"* (What's happening/What's up?). Or say *"Oye"* ("Hey" or "Listen") *or "Hija/Hijo"* (son/daughter), as in "My mom was talking to me last night and she said *"Mi hija,* don't stay up too late—go to bed by 10:00!"

There is no hard-and-fast rule when it comes to using English or Spanish. Think about your product and service and who your primary potential customer is. Let's go back to the banking example. Financial services can be complex. It's not an "easy" product or service to market. People have lots of questions, and the subject matter—their money—is a very serious and personal one. If you're targeting less acculturated Hispanics, you'd certainly want to use Spanish, not only because it's their preferred language, but because they're more likely to better comprehend the details of the information in their native language.

If you're promoting a local kids' soccer league, you may want to promote your league bilingually. The kids most likely playing in the league will probably speak and read English, but their parents may be more comfortable with Spanish. In that case, a good solution would be a flyer with English on one side and Spanish on the other.

For certain industries, even "Spanglish" may be the way to go, although language purists may cringe. (In the movie *Tortilla Soup*, about a single father raising his three daughters, the daughters repeatedly lapse into "Spanglish" at the dinner table and the father repeatedly admonishes, "English or Spanish! One or the other!"). The use of "Spanglish" is becoming more common in industries with products aimed at young adults and teens. The telecommunications and electronics industries, as well as fast food and soft drinks, frequently use "Spanglish" because they know that's how kids today actually talk, and they want to be as authentic, as *relevant,* as possible.

Fanta is a soft drink brand that is hugely popular in Latin America, particularly Mexico. It makes sense that, if you're foreign-born and living in the United States, you're probably familiar with Fanta. And Fanta wants to keep you as a customer and not lose you to Coke or Pepsi or Mountain Dew. Teens drink more soft drinks than any other age group. So Fanta has created campaigns targeted to Hispanic teens. One ad features sexy, gorgeous dancers in colorful shorts and go-go boots, holding various flavors of Fanta and singing, *"¿Quieres? Quieres?"* (You want some? You want some?) Then the voiceover in the ad is in English. And the ad runs on English-language programming, such as MTV and VH1. That's a use of "Spanglish" that is highly targeted and appropriate for what they're selling and to whom.

If your potential customer is more acculturated, it makes sense to market to them in English. Or if what you're selling transcends racial, ethnic, and linguistic values, English is likely the best means of communicating your message broadly.

An example of this is the Toyota Prius. The Prius, the first hybrid vehicle using gas and electric technology, is marketed heavily in California. This is because California is home to many people who are strong supporters of ecology, conservation, and being "green." In fact, the green movement started on the West Coast. California is also home to more Hispanics than any other state—one in three people who live in California are Hispanic. So Toyota markets the

Prius heavily in California, and they do it in English, but they feature people in their ads who are White, Black, Hispanic, and Asian. This is because the Prius is marketed not to certain racial or ethnic groups, but to a consumer with strongly held beliefs and values about ecology.

Spanish or English? Both? It all depends. There is no one right answer. But with careful thought about what you're trying to market, and to whom, the best approach will reveal itself.

STEP 3: TRANSCREATION, NOT TRANSLATION

OK, so you've made your business Latino-ready and Latino-friendly. Let's say you've also identified that your high-potential Hispanic customer is less acculturated, and therefore, is Spanish-dominant. You know you are going to need to market to them in Spanish. But wait—before you go running off to a translation service or, heaven forbid, use one of those Internet translation services to have your brochure translated, let me introduce you to the concept of *transcreation*. Transcreation means expressing something in a culturally relevant manner, not simply doing a word-forword translation. Let me give you an example. In English, there is an expression: "the bottom line," which can mean several things, including "in summary" or "the final outcome" or "company profit." It's a widely used phrase and often shows up in business ads and marketing communications. (e.g., *This mega sale ends Saturday! You'll save hundreds of dollars! The bottom line is: don't wait!)* In Spanish, there is no such expression as "the bottom line." Sure, you can write the words in Spanish—*la linea baja* (the line below)—but they don't mean anything. There is no meaning attached to those three words. So if you were translating from English to Spanish, you'd end up with a phrase that is completely meaningless. Kind of like stringing three words together in English (e.g., railing leaf hot). Those are three English words, yes, and you can read them, but together, they don't mean anything. In the case of "the bottom line," a transcreation of that phrase would probably be something along the lines of *"el punto es . . . "* (the point is . . .). Not very likely that a translation software program on the Web would offer that as an alternative to "the bottom line."

OK, so you'll take the advertising copy to a translator, right? Not so fast. While a translation service will provide you with a grammatically correct translation, once again, it may not have the correct meaning you want, or it may not be culturally relevant. Here's a real example: the "Got Milk?" ad campaign is, in my opinion, one of the most clever and memorable of my lifetime. I say this because they managed to take a pretty standard, boring product (milk) and make it really compelling through the use of famous athletes, entertainers, and celebrities, all wearing milk mustaches. It's something most of us can relate to, because most of us probably had a milk mustache a few times in our childhoods. It's universally appealing. And the simplicity of the message, "Got Milk?" reminds us to drink milk frequently. But if you take that simple message and translate it—exactly—into Spanish, the phrase is *"¿Tiene leche?"* (Do you have milk?). The problem is, that phrase means "are you lactating?" That's hardly the meaning the milk marketers were going for! So, what did they do? The ads in Spanish for milk say *"Más leche"* (*more milk*). That's a great example of how transcreation succeeds where translation fails.

Another reason to use transcreation is for cultural relevance. Just because you can take something in English and express it in Spanish doesn't mean it will have meaningful relevance. As mentioned in Chapter Five, a bank in Houston asked us to translate their product brochures into Spanish. One of their brochures was for personal loans. The copy in the brochure said, "Why would you want to take out a personal loan? For that motorcycle or RV (recreational vehicle) that you've always wanted to buy." As we reviewed the copy, we knew that simply translating those sentences wouldn't be that meaningful to their Hispanic target. We knew that Hispanics do not index high in the purchase of either motorcycles or RVs. So we recommended to the client that we modify the copy in Spanish to read, "Why would you want to take out a personal loan? For that family computer you've wanted to buy or that family vacation you've wanted to take." What we did was convey the same *meaning* (personal reasons why someone would want to take out a loan), but we expressed it in a *culturally relevant way*. That's transcreation—creating a meaningful message in another language that expresses the thought of the original message.

You may be asking yourself how you go about finding someone who can transcreate for you. Your best bet is to use a *marketing* firm that specializes in the culture you're trying to reach, rather than use a translation company. Whether you're trying to reach a Hispanic audience, Chinese audience, or any other target that speaks a language other than yours, a marketing firm will look at the message and be able to offer transcreation and insights into what to say and why. You may pay slightly more for this service than you would a translation company, but it will be well worth it. (Translation services usually charge by the word. Marketing firms typically charge an hourly rate. Either should be able to provide you a free quote for the work you need, and it's usually not expensive).

To find a specialized marketing firm or ad agency, the Internet is your best bet for a search. By Googling a phrase such as "Vietnamese advertising," a long list of companies will appear, and many tout their "translation" services. Don't be afraid of the word *translation* in this sense. On these companies' web sites, they use *translation* because the average person does not know what *transcreation* means. But trust me—they will transcreate your work, not just translate it.

What if using a marketing firm just isn't in the budget? If you find yourself in this situation and need to create a Spanish message but simply have little or no budget, then keep your message as basic, clear and free of idioms and expressions as possible. In other words, let's say you're a local tire dealer. Don't create an ad that says "the best in the West!" or "We're unbeatable! We'll match any competitor's deal." Keep it simple and use phrases that have no room for interpretation. Use phrases like "Low prices. Open late. Monday–Friday 7 AM to 9 PM." These are phrases that require no transcreation because they are simple, clear statements.

STEP 4: NEW PRODUCTS, NEW HOURS, NEW UNIFORMS

Earlier in this chapter, we covered how some companies are modifying their product offerings to better meet the needs of the Hispanic market. Whether it's Bud Lime beer (inspired by Hispanics' tendency to squeeze a lime into their beer) or cinnamon-flavored toothpaste (in the United States, fresh breath and a clean mouth are associated with "mint," but in Latin America, fresh breath is associated with cinnamon and other intense flavors, such as sour apple, citrus, and vanilla-flavored toothpastes), brands of all kinds are examining their products and exploring opportunities to grow business by making modifications. A local furniture retailer told me he'd received a bright red couch (his inventory is ordered by corporate headquarters) and he was panicked because he wasn't sure he'd be able to sell it. "Neutrals are what sells," he told me. "Beige, brown, black, gray, and olive. But I didn't have to worry. Within two days, I'd sold that red couch to a Hispanic family. They liked the bright color and wanted to add some 'pop' to their living room. In fact, we have such a large Hispanic population here, I asked headquarters to send me more red couches!"

In addition to thinking about how your products may be customized or modified for the Hispanic market, consider hours of operation as well. If you are a retailer or you offer a professional service (financial services, legal services, realtor, etc.), you need to be open for business when Hispanics want to, and are able to, do business with you. For some retailers, this may present a problem, because they may be closed on Sundays, yet that's the day when many Hispanic families will shop and look at products together because that's the day that, for many families, *Papá* isn't working.

A home builder of entry-level homes wanted to attract more Hispanic home buyers. They were Latino-ready: they had a Spanish-speaking agent who did a great job working with their Hispanic buyers. Because their homes were priced at the entry point to the industry, their clientele was primarily first-time home buyers. Buying your first house can be very exciting . . . and overwhelming. Now imagine what it's like to go through that process in a new country. This home builder understood this anxiety and the millions of questions a prospective home buyer has. The builder wanted to be Latino-friendly and really educate their buyers and sort of "hold their hand" through the complex and confusing process of buying a first home.

They decided to hold free classes at the local library on Tuesday nights. The topic was "What you need to know to buy your first home" and the class was conducted in Spanish by Julia, their Spanish-speaking agent. They hired our firm to help design and create the literature that they would be handing out at the classes. When we had to determine what time the classes should be held, it was agreed that 7:30 PM would be the "advertised" start time. We knew there may be a few people who might run late and the thought was that the class could start as late as 8 PM and still conclude by 9 PM, leaving plenty of time for questions and answers. Because Julia knew the clientele so well, she knew this start time would work. It gave working parents a chance to get off work, feed their family dinner, and still attend a class on an important topic. The result? The classes were packed and their sales to Hispanic home buyers increased 12 percent in the first four months of the program.

Another example of hours modification is a large, national fast food company that had, until recent years, only been open for lunch and dinner, not breakfast. The fast food arena is a highly competitive one and this brand wanted their share of the breakfast market. Research shows that men eat more fast food than women and that Hispanic men consume more fast food than men of any other race or ethnicity. This led the company to our door, where they asked for a meeting with us to discuss the launch of their new breakfast sandwich, their first foray into the breakfast world. As we talked with the senior VP of marketing about the launch, we asked what time the company planed to open for business in the morning. He replied "6:30 AM" and my staff started to chuckle (politely), and they all shook their heads. "What's wrong with 6:30?, the client asked. "Too late," all the employees responded. Liliana, our top executive, stated, "The Hispanic men that you want are hard-working, blue-collar guys. A lot of them work in construction. They need to be on the job site by 6:45 AM, so if they're going to grab breakfast on the way to work, they need to be able to get it by 6 AM; 5:30 AM would actually be even better." The senior VP of marketing nodded. He got it. And when the company launched its breakfast menu, it was open for business at 6 AM.

New products and new hours may be important when marketing to Hispanics. Another tool in your "toolbox" can be demonstrating sensitivity to cultural nuances. I live in Dallas, Texas, and in the summer, the temperatures are in the 100s almost every day. Imagine working for a car dealership and showing vehicles to prospective buyers in that heat—walking around for hours on asphalt, showing car after car, with no shade. It's brutal. People here adapt—many dealerships allow their sales force to wear khaki shorts and polo shirts in the summer. It's practical. However, one of the largest and most successful dealerships in the country is here and in speaking with the sales manager one day, he mentioned that their Hispanic salesmen do not dress that way in the summer. He went on to explain that "in Latin America, and especially Mexico, men do not wear shorts. Shorts are for little boys. It's a school uniform for little boys. Our clientele is going to come in here and spend $35,000 or more on a new car or truck. They expect to speak with a professional. And that professional shouldn't be wearing shorts." It was a significant cultural insight and the dealership requested that their Hispanic sales associates wear khaki slacks and a collared polo shirt or collared shirt with no tie. It was a practical solution and one with cultural relevance. The sales associates readily complied because they knew that the more relaxed their customers are and the more trust their customers place in them as sales professionals, the greater their ability to close the sale.

STEP 5: CUSTOMER SERVICE IS YOUR SECRET WEAPON

The last and final step in your Hispanic marketing plan is to consider a few customer service nuances. Three key values of Hispanic culture are relationships, pleasing others, and being polite and respectful. These values manifest themselves in service, which is a cornerstone of Hispanic interaction. Whether it's in a professional setting or at a restaurant or a store, Hispanic culture is exceedingly warm and polite, and great emphasis is placed on providing exceptional customer service. Here are several tips for providing your Hispanic customers with service that will keep them coming back for more:

- Always make eye contact and greet customers with a warm and welcoming smile.
- Be patient with questions. Some Hispanic customers may be unfamiliar with a product, service contract, or terminology, and they will appreciate be given all the time that they need to ask questions.
- Show respect. We all want respect. We know when we're getting it and when we're not.
- Show respect toward the elderly. Hispanic culture values and respects the elderly and often Hispanic customers will make

comments such as, "I really liked the salesperson. She was very attentive to my mother and spent a lot of time talking with her and answering her questions."

- Consider the entire family. For many Hispanics, shopping and doing business is a family affair. The whole family will run errands together and make purchase decisions together; even the kids get a "vote" on what kind of washing machine to buy! Be prepared for this and don't overlook the children. Whether it's extra seating in the waiting room of an office or having balloons for the kids, acknowledge the whole family and make sure everyone is comfortable.

- Take your time. Good customer service takes time and Hispanics value relationships. The business exchange is not as "transactional" for Hispanics; it's about the relationship that is formed. Be warm and personal. Ask about their families, where they're from (if they're foreign-born) and other engaging topics.

Great customer service is your secret weapon. It will cover a multitude of sins and errors. A well-known, national fast food chain did a study of customer satisfaction scores among their Hispanic and non-Hispanic customers. They found that when Hispanic customers felt they received good service, they were far more forgiving of errors in their order than non-Hispanics. "Forgot the fries in my order? Gave me a hamburger instead of a cheeseburger? It's OK—the lady at the counter was really nice" was the attitude among Hispanic customers. Non-Hispanic customers were very harsh and critical of every mistake, regardless of whether they'd received good personal service. Research also shows that Hispanics are willing to drive greater distances to get that personal service.

Providing great customer service is always a good idea for *every* customer. For your Hispanic customers, it's often more important than price, speed, or location. It's the secret weapon in your arsenal and one that costs very little but means everything.

The Hispanic population in the United States will continue to be a major force in marketing and in the economy for decades to come. Your business can grow and prosper by targeting Hispanics with meaningful marketing, the right products, and exceptional customer service.

CHAPTER TWELVE ⟫
African-Americans

A Large and Lucrative Customer Base

Although people of color live all over the world, this chapter is focused on how to market to people of color in the United States. Why? Because the United States tends to have more of a racial divide than European countries, Canada, and other places in the world. Although race relations continue to improve in the United States, there still exists a "difference" in the U.S. African-American consumer market compared to what is commonly called the "general market" (non-African-American).

African-American marketing really began gaining momentum in the 1990s, when the consumer purchasing power of Blacks became documented through research. Studies were published that showed that not only were Blacks a large and lucrative market segment, but a loyal one as well. Brands that reached out to African-Americans through targeted marketing efforts received strong sales results and grew their market share. Today, there are marketing firms that are highly specialized and dedicated almost exclusively to African-American marketing, and more companies and brands devote a significant portion of their marketing budgets to African-American efforts. Why? Quite simply, it works. It makes money. Here are some statistics about the African-American market in the United States worth noting:

- The African-American population numbered 42 million in 2010, accounting for 14 percent of the U.S. population.
- Nearly half of African-Americans have at least some college experience, and 38 percent have a bachelor's degree.
- Sixty-eight percent of the nation's African-American households own their home.
- Twelve percent of the African-American population is between the ages of 18 and 24.
- Thirty-five percent of African-Americans are employed as managers or professionals.
- African-Americans spend 73 percent more time than the average person in religious activities.
- More than half of African-Americans (54 percent) live in the South, where they account for 20 percent of the population.[1]

Figure 12.1 shows the top ten African-American markets in the United States, based on population size and percentage of the market that is African-American.

If you want to grow your customer base with African-American consumers, there are several things you should know.

First, there is no one "African-American consumer profile," just as there is no one "White profile," or "Asian profile," or "Hispanic profile." We are all different, and most of the categories that marketers develop to define us do a pretty superficial job of doing so, at best.

---

[1] The New Strategist Editions. *Racial and Ethnic Diversity: Asians, Blacks, Hispanics, Native Americans, and Whites.* 6th edition. New York: New Strategist, 2009; Synovate 2010.

| Top African-American Markets by Population ||||
Market	Population (in millions)	Market	African American %
New York, NY	3.9	Greenwood/Greenville, NC	67%
Atlanta, GA	1.9	Jackson, MS	47%
Chicago, IL	1.9	Montgomery, AL	42%
Washington DC	1.6	Memphis, TN	42%
Philadelphia, PA	1.6	Columbia, SC	41%
Los Angeles, CA	1.4	Albany, GA	40%
Detroit, MI	1.2	Meridian, MS	40%
Houston, TX	1.1	Columbus, GA	39%
Dallas/Ft. Worth, TX	1.0	Macon, GA	37%
Miami, FL	1.0	Augusta, GA	37%

FIGURE 12.1   Top African-American markets in the United States

Source: Synovate's 2010 U.S. Diversity Markets Report

However, there are some generalities and overarching insights and consumer comments that I believe will help you in developing a solid African-American marketing plan.

INSIGHT 1: SHOW PEOPLE OF COLOR WHEN TARGETING PEOPLE OF COLOR

One of the most powerful insights that I've come across was a comment made in an African-American focus group. The group was comprised of African-American men and women of different ages, different backgrounds, and from different cities, and the discussion topic was advertising and how African-Americans were portrayed in ads and how the group felt about marketing to blacks. One woman in the group, Kim Edwards, a successful business owner, stated that she was drawn to almost any ad where she could "fit in." I asked her what she meant by that, and she explained, saying, "As Blacks, we haven't been in ads for very long. It's only recently that we've started seeing images of people who look like us in ads. We've been absent from marketing efforts for so long that we're trained to 'get in where we fit in.' By that, I mean that, if I see an ad for a product and there's no person in the ad, I can picture that product being for me. I can see myself using that product. Or if there's a person who's brown or Black, I can "fit myself into that ad." But if there's a person in the ad and they're White, then I don't feel as much of a connection, because I don't look like that." When Edwards made this comment, the entire focus group came alive and nodded their agreement. Others in the group shared similar feelings: "We've been overlooked for so long. We immediately identify when we see a person of color in an ad, because for the longest time, we haven't been in many ads."

When you think about it, this is such a simple truth that it's hard to believe it's an insight. But we humans always relate to others just like us. That's why ads for retirement and financial planning always feature people in their 50s and 60s—because retirement is very much on the minds of people that age. The target audience will more readily identify this as "an ad or product that's relevant to me" if they see someone in the ad who looks like they could be facing the same concerns as they, the viewers, are. So it's no surprise that most African-Americans will take note of an ad or marketing efforts that features African-Americans. In fact, a research study by Yankelovich shows that 70 percent of African-Americans say it's very important to them to see African-Americans in ads.

INSIGHT 2: DIVERSITY IN SKIN TONE IS VERY IMPORTANT

You may have noticed that I use the terms *Black* and *people of color* as well as *African-American*. This is because, all over the world, diversity in skin color is no longer confined to shades of white, black, or brown. There is a range of skin color, from very light to very dark, and everything in between. Additionally, as societies have become more mobile and integrated, it's not uncommon for people to be of mixed race. Those who are biracial or multiracial often identify themselves as a "person of color" rather than "Black" or "White." "Person of color" more aptly captures a much broader definition of color than Black or White. In fact, a young woman in an African-American focus group stated that she liked a particular ad for sneakers just because it featured a young girl who she said "looks like my sister." The young woman stated, "I have one Black parent and one White parent, so my sister and I are mixed and we're very light-skinned African-Americans. With freckles! But the girl in this ad looks just like my sister, with brown wavy hair and freckles and a light brown complexion. And she has a smile just like my sister, so it immediately caught my eye." Another woman in the same focus group added, "You don't have to show only Black people in order to connect with me. We'll get into anything other than White people. Most of us have people in our families or social circles who are very light-skinned or very black and every color in between. So if you show any range of brown or black, we can relate. We just can't relate all that well to the White model." If you feature people of color in your marketing efforts, make an effort to show diversity in skin tone.

INSIGHT 3: DON'T EVEN USE PEOPLE IN ADS AT ALL—LEAVE IT OPEN TO INTERPRETATION

A great alternative to featuring people in ads is *not* featuring people in ads at all. Sometimes, this can be the best approach, particularly if you have a visually appealing product, a product that needs little or no explanation or you have a lot to say. The reason this can be a good tactic is that this approach doesn't exclude anyone. "If no one's in the ad, we don't have to try to fit in it," says Karen Eaton, an executive who works with international companies and teams. "Show me your product or tell me how your product or service offers me a solution for my life—that's what will sell me."

INSIGHT 4: KEEP IT REAL

Time and time again in consumer panels and focus groups, the issue of "keeping it real" comes up. In the busy, connected world we live in, ad messages come at us every minute of every day. We're bombarded and we're being "pitched" all the time. So it makes sense that this wears on us and, as consumers, we gravitate toward that which we find to be authentic and real. Target department stores does a great job of this; their ads feature attractive models of all different races and colors, but they're relatable because they portray those models doing everyday, "real" things. They look like they could be me or you, so Target ads feel relevant to us because they showcase real life. Compare that with Baby Phat—a clothing,

FIGURE 12.2   Target Advertisement

fashion, and fragrance brand that positions itself as very bold and fashion forward. The clothes are cutting edge and youthful, and for most people, completely unwearable. But it's the ads for Baby Phat that are over the top. They scream "look at me," and nothing about them is real or believable. The ads feature founder Kimora Lee Simmons, and her image has been extensively retouched (see Figures 12.2 and 12.3). In real life, she's a curvy woman. In the ads, her legs and thighs have been retouched and whittled to skinny. Despite the fact that her products and brand are heavily marketed to women of color, many stated in a focus group that they disliked the ads because they are so "artificial." Comments included, "Nobody dresses like that. Nobody looks like that. Even Kimora herself doesn't look like that!"

Compare that with the woman featured in an ad for Roots of Nature hair products (see Figure 12.4). She's an attractive woman, with a chic haircut and her hair looks healthy and shiny. More importantly, however, she looks *real*. Yes, she's attractive, but she's not a supermodel. And yes, she has a great haircut, but it's also the kind of style that real, everyday women can, and would, wear. It's not hair extensions. It's not a wig. And it's not a completely unrealistic look— it's the kind of look that contemporary, stylish African-American women have or want to have. The woman in the ad is utterly relatable. She looks real.

FIGURE 12.3   Baby Phat Advertisement

"We're constantly portrayed as something we're not," said one focus group participant. "We're either portrayed as the Black woman with attitude (think "Florida," the TV character in the old TV show *Good Times*) or as light-skinned. Or the oversexed, hot chick with no substance. Why don't more marketers just show us real people?"

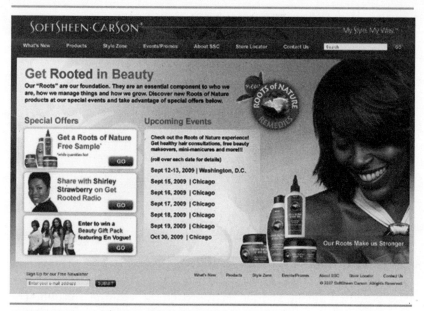

FIGURE 12.4   Roots of Nature Advertisement

INSIGHT 5: YOU DON'T HAVE TO MAKE IT "BROWN" TO APPEAL TO AFRICAN-AMERICANS

As mentioned in Chapter 9, there used to be an expression in marketing that, in order to sell something to women, you had to "pink it or shrink it." The thought was that women would only buy "girly" products. That's not only been proven untrue, it's also really outdated thinking. The same is true for products and ads that are targeted to African-Americans. It seems that a lot of companies and brands think they need to "brown" the package to let African-American consumers know that "this product is targeted to you!" And many African-Americans say that this is an insulting approach. "Sure, I want advertisers to recognize me and want my business, but you don't need to make the package brown to show me it's for me," is a direct quote from a focus group participant.

Here's an example: African-Americans are a very valuable consumer group for the skin care industry. Because most people of color have drier skin than Whites, moisturizing daily is a must to keep skin looking its best. Therefore, skin care is a large market for African-American targeted products. Let's look at the contrast between how two skin

FIGURE 12.5   Dove Box

care brands, Vaseline and Dove, approach this consumer group. The Vaseline ad features a person of color, but "just in case we didn't get it, they've also made the product packages brown!" says Melissa Lewis, a social services executive. "Dove, on the other hand, keeps their package normal, but prominently features 'shea butter,' so I know it's for me" (see Figure 12.5). When asked why shea butter means "it's for me," Melissa explained, "Shea butter is from Africa—it is a very moisturizing, natural ingredient that has been used for thousands of years on skin. Plus, the look of the packaging is soothing, the soap looks creamy and moisturizing—I know this product will soothe and smooth my skin. You don't have to "hit me over the head" that this product is for African-Americans. I get it."

Another example of the "brown" approach that consumers found off-putting is for Pantene's Relaxed & Natural Collection (see Figure 12.6). "The very fact that this line is called "Relaxed & Natural" tells us it's made for African-American hair," said one panelist. "You don't need to put it in a brown bottle, too!"

INSIGHT 6: PEOPLE OF COLOR ASPIRE TO MORE THAN JUST SPORTS, MUSIC, AND FASHION

Most advertising and marketing is aspirational. We all aspire to certain things: greater beauty, more status, more wealth, greater health, more

FIGURE 12.6   Pantene Advertisement

happiness, and so on. Marketers know this and create ads that they hope will connect with us on an aspirational level. The idea is that you may not live like this now, but perhaps you *could,* if only you wore a certain fragrance, had a certain type of computer, or stayed in certain hotels. And because for decades, African-Americans achieved success in the United States through fashion, sports, or music, many marketers think those are the only "paths of aspiration" for African-Americans. Many ads targeted to African-Americans are centered on hip, cool, youth-oriented images with loud colors and overt sex appeal or macho sports appeal. This is a shame because, of course, there are more substantive things to aspire to, like education and professional success and personal and family well-being. Take this ad for Mercedes-Benz, for example (see Figure 12.7). It is an excellent example of aspirational advertising. After all, no one really *needs* a luxury car. A luxury car is *earned,* through hard work and sacrifice. This ad clearly showcases the success and status of achievement that Mercedes-Benz represents, and

FIGURE 12.7   Mercedes Benz Advertisement

it also is targeted to people of color. The copy reads: "When they said Ben wouldn't make it, he stood his ground. When they said he wouldn't finish school, he stood his ground. When he doubted himself, his mom made him stand his ground. Today, Dr. Ben Carson is one of the world's top pediatric neurosurgeons. And when he's not using his gifted hands to save lives, he's driving his Mercedes. Who knew standing still could take someone so far?"

Here's what makes this ad so great: it is completely authentic in its portrayal of the ultimate success in life. Dr. Ben Carson performed the first surgery that successfully separated twins joined at the tops of their heads. And while that is truly amazing, what's even more amazing are the odds that he overcame to achieve his success. His mother was a third-grade dropout who could barely read. Ben Carson fell behind in school and nearly flunked out. Determined to turn her son's school performance around, his mother eliminated his TV time and refused to let him go outside to play until he finished his homework. She made him read two library books a week and required him to give her written reports on what he'd read, even though she could barely read what he'd written. His grades improved, and he began soaring academically. The ad makes reference to hardship and personal sacrifice. It makes reference to the fact that he was raised by a single mom. It makes reference to the struggle and self-doubt that many people face growing up and trying to get through school, especially with hardworking parents who work long hours to keep a family going. It's aspirational, not because it promises you that you'll become a gorgeous celebrity or star athlete, but because it shows that hard work, perseverance, and support can take you very far. And isn't that what driving a luxury car is about? It's a statement of achievement and personal success. This ad uses aspiration to sell the product, but it does so in a believable, real way, because it *is* real.

INSIGHT 7: GET INVOLVED AND SUPPORT THE COMMUNITY

As in the previous chapters on immigrants and Hispanics, I recommend that if you want to target the African-American community, get involved in the needs of the community and find a way to contribute. Whether it's through educational, family, or health efforts; faith organizations; or expanding community resources, you can successfully market to people of color by showing that you're committed to the community. With *all* diversity marketing, it's important that the target consumer feels recognized and valued for who they are, not just the size of their wallet. You don't just want to sell someone your product or service today; you want to keep them as a customer for life. And becoming involved in the community is a tangible way to show your support and ongoing appreciation of a consumer group.

Your efforts to become involved don't have to be large or expensive. Start locally. Look around, ask around, and find out what's needed. Perhaps a local children's sports team needs jerseys. You could sponsor them. Perhaps a playground needs some repairs or a school needs a few new computers. Maybe having a booth at a local health fair or festival is a way to get information about your company, product, or service out while helping support the fair or festival. Becoming involved in the African-American community will give you insights into what your potential customers want and how you can best provide it to them.

THE QUESTION ISN'T WHETHER THEY'LL SOAR; IT'S HOW HIGH.

WITH THE POWER OF AN EDUCATION, THE SKY IS THE LIMIT.
At Southwest Airlines,° we're committed to supporting education-related programs that
help thousands of children each year—like Southwest's Adopt-A-Pilot, National Urban
League Black Executive Exchange Program, and the Tom Joyner Foundation° to name a
few. With a little help, today's African American youth will become tomorrow's leaders, and
that's why we celebrate Black History Month yearround. Visit **southwest.com/blackhistory.**

SOUTHWEST.COM

FIGURE 12.8   Southwest Airlines Advertisement

This ad for Southwest Airlines shows that the company is involved
in the African-American community with scholarships, mentoring
programs, and executive leadership programs (see Figure 12.8). Of
course, they want to sell plane tickets to African-Americans. But
Southwest is building loyalty among fliers by tangibly demonstrating
that people of color are important to them, and not just important to
their bottom line.

INSIGHT 8: FOOD, MUSIC, AND SOCIALIZING ARE CENTRAL TO AFRICAN-AMERICAN CULTURE

It seems that every culture revolves around food and music, and African-American culture is no different. Being with friends, family. and loved ones is an important part of African-American life, so presenting opportunities that weave these together can boost your marketing efforts.

I know of a small restaurant owner who wanted to attract more African-Americans and people of color to his restaurant (the restaurant owner is White). He held a special night of jazz and blues music, and gave patrons the opportunity to sample special foods and socialize in a casual manner. He promoted the evening with inexpensive flyers distributed in high-density African-American neighborhoods, including salons and barbershops, inviting people to stop by and try out his restaurant. It worked. Customers came, enjoyed the food and the atmosphere, and told their friends about it. Today, he estimates that nearly half his customer base is African-American, whereas before he made any effort, it had been about 10 percent.

"Connect with us through music," advises Percy Bryant III, owner of AMP, a marketing and promotions firm that specializes in urban and African-American marketing. "Bring us together with music and food and the opportunity to mingle and socialize and you'll reach us and build loyalty." What if you don't have a restaurant? Suppose your business is house painting, for example? In that case, utilize the themes of togetherness and socializing and your message will resonate with the African-American community. For example, create an ad or flyer that shows a family of color enjoying a meal in their kitchen or backyard and laughing and loving being together. Your copy could state something along the lines of *"Your home is where your loved ones are and you want the best for your loved ones. Call ABC House Painters for a free, no obligation estimate on painting your home. Reliable, dependable, satisfaction guaranteed. Fair prices."*

Utilizing imagery of people of color socializing and enjoying a meal together will resonate. And the rest of the message just needs to be clear, honest, and sincere. Which leads me to the next insight.

INSIGHT 9: DON'T TAKE ADVANTAGE OF AFRICAN-AMERICAN CUSTOMERS

I shouldn't even have to write this as an insight, but this comment came up in so many consumer focus groups that it needs to be addressed. Many African-Americans feel that some businesses exploit them, or try to. They say that prices may be unusually high or that terms differ for them. For example, one focus group participant tells of a company that did window-washing and quoted him a higher price for washing his windows than his neighbor (who is not African-American) was charged. His neighbor's house is an identical floor plan with the same number of windows. Furthermore, his neighbor paid the company when the job was completed. But for the African-American homeowner, when the company provided the estimate, they also asked for a deposit up front "to get started," with the balance due at the end of the job. "I guess they thought I might not pay them," said the panelist. "How insulting is that?"

Here are some Do's and Don'ts for reaching the African-American market or people of color:

DO

- Do be honest, straightforward, and consistent in your pricing and business practices.
- Do be dependable. Show respect for others' time and make sure your product or service is doing what you've promised.
- Do ask for referrals when your customers are happy and satisfied.
- Do be sincere in your efforts. Don't just try to make money off the African-American consumer. Cultivate an ongoing, loyal relationship between the customer and your business and the money will follow.
- Do get involved in the African-American community and support the community.
- Do connect with the community where they are: neighborhoods, salons, barbershops, churches, restaurants, and clubs.
- Do explore African-American media. In most markets, there are newspapers, radio stations, and web sites that are targeted specifically to the Black community. These can be excellent avenues for your marketing efforts.

DON'T

- Don't be pushy and try to oversell. Explain your product or service, tout its features and benefits, and let the consumer make an informed decision.
- Don't try to be too cool or hip. Just be who you are.
- "Don't try to connect with me by telling me you've got a Black friend." This comment was echoed in many consumer focus groups. "I don't care if you've got a Black friend. Just connect with me by being a good business with a product or service I need and fair prices."
- Don't make assumptions about financial status. "It's so insulting when someone assumes that I have weak credit or don't care about the stock market just because I'm Black. I make good money, I have investments and I take care of my finances just like anyone else."
- Don't try to connect on a superficial level. An African-American woman tells of a salesperson at an appliance store who tried to make small talk with her by asking her if she liked the music of Beyonce and Jay Z. "It felt so weird and superficial to me to have this salesman chat with me about music because I know he was doing it just because I'm Black. I would have much rather discussed the features of the washing machine."

The African-American consumer and people of color can be your best customers. They want to know about your products and services. They want your recognition, your respect, and your marketing efforts. Use these insights to guide your marketing efforts and watch your sales grow.

In the next chapter, we'll cover marketing to Asians—a market segment with the highest household income group of any race or ethnicity.

CHAPTER THIRTEEN ⟫
Asians and Asian-Americans

The Highest Household Income of Any Racial or Ethnic Group

From a marketing perspective, the strength of the Asian population is pretty irrefutable. It's the largest population in the world, numbering nearly 8 billion as of this writing, and in the United States and Canada, Asian-Americans have the highest household income of any race or ethnicity. So whether you're trying to sell shoes in China or home mortgages in Canada, learning about the Asian market is worth your time.

So what is the definition of Asian? It varies from country to country around the world, but the most common definition is a person who descends from East Asia, South Asia, and Southeast Asia. Here are some (but not all) of the groups that are considered to be Asian:

Chinese	Filipino	Yemeni
Pakistani	Korean	Thai
Vietnamese	Lebanese	Burmese
Iranian	Sri Lankan	Sakha
Japanese	Afghani	Nepali
Syrian	Iraqi	Malaysian
Cambodian	Bangladeshi	Jordanian
Palestinian	Laotian	Tibetan
Taiwanese	Indonesian	Mongolian
Saudi	Singaporian	

THE U.S. ASIAN POPULATION

Current estimates indicate that about 5 percent of the U.S. population report themselves as having either full or partial Asian heritage (approximately 15 million people). The largest ethnic subgroups are Chinese, Filipinos, Indians, Vietnamese, Koreans, and Japanese. Other sizable groups are Cambodian/Khmer, Pakistanis, Laotians, Hmong, and Thais. Figure 13.1 shows the percentage of the composition of several key groups of Asian-Americans.

The Asian-American population is extremely attractive to marketers. In addition to the high household income of Asian-Americans, they also have the lowest poverty rate and highest educational

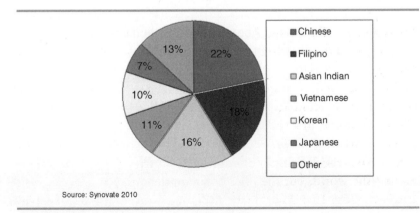

Source: Synovate 2010

FIGURE 13.1   U.S. Asian Composition

attainment levels of any race or ethnicity. Asians are the third largest minority group in the United States, behind Hispanics and African-Americans. They're also very young, with an average age of just 34 years. In terms of income and buying power, here's a breakout of average household income for key subsegments:

Asian Indian	$90,000
Filipinos	$80,000
Chinese	$65,000
Vietnamese	$55,000
Korean	$54,000

Geographically, the top places in the United States for marketing to Asians are California and New York. This is because there are large concentrations of population, combined with the aforementioned buying power, and also many Asian media outlets. Additionally, Asian youth tend to fit a profile of exactly what marketers hunger for: tech-savvy, early adopters who value style and function and who watch trends carefully. They're also very connected to friends and family, both online and off.

In Chapter 10, an acculturation model with four segments or "mind-sets" was presented. For the Asian market, GlobalHue, a globally renowned marketing firm that specializes in Asian and other multicultural marketing segments, created a three-tiered model of acculturation (see Figure 13.2).

Overview: Acculturation Spectrum within an Asian Family

2ⁿᵈ Gen U.S.Born

1.5 Generation Foreign born, but immigrated at an early age Skews Youth/Young Adults

1ˢᵗ Generation Foreign Born Skews Older/Parents

Early Adopters
Translation Bridge
Brand Pushers
More Confidence

Traditional
Entrepreneurial
Comfortable with global brands
Co-signer

FIGURE 13.2   Acculturation Spectrum within an Asian Family

So what do you need to know to effectively reach the Asian market for your products or services? This chapter presents some key things to consider and keep in mind.

STEP 1: EVALUATE THE "SIZE OF THE PRIZE"

If your product or service is sold in an area with a large Asian population, you don't want to miss out on the opportunity to reach this market. Figure 13.3 shows the top Asian markets in the United States, by population as well as percentage of the total population. You can see that if you're doing business in one of these markets, you certainly don't want to overlook the Asian consumer. In San Francisco, for example, one in five people are Asian. You'd absolutely want to reach this consumer and have them be aware of your product or service.

Do your homework and determine if the size of the Asian population in a given area merits developing an Asian marketing plan. Don't just review population numbers—look at percentage of the population as well. For example, you might not think of Millbourne, Pennsylvania, as a major Asian market. There are only 943 people who live in this town. Yet 54 percent are Asian. So if I lived and worked in Millbourne and had a small business, and more than half of the town is Asian, I'd certainly value the "size of the prize" and make every effort to reach the local Asian community in a meaningful way.

Top U.S. Asian Markets by Population			
Market	Population (000s)	Market	Asian %
Los Angeles, CA	2,540.5	Honolulu, HI	55%
New York, NY	2,184.5	San Francisco/Oakland/San Jose, CA	24%
San Francisco/Oakland/San Jose, CA	1,839.8	Los Angeles, CA	13%
Honolulu, HI	820.1	Sacramento/Stockton/Modesto,	12%
Chicago, IL	626.6	San Diego, CA	12%
Washington, DC	579.1	Seattle/Tacoma, WA	10%
Sacramento/Stockton/Modesto, CA	567.5	New York, NY	9%
Seattle/Tacoma, WA	531.1	Las Vegas, NV	8%
Philadelphia, PA	402.9	Washington, DC	8%
San Diego, CA	400.7	Fresno/Visalia, CA	7%

FIGURE 13.3   Top U.S. Asian Markets by Population

Source: Synovate's 2010 U.S. Diversity Markets Report

STEP 2: LEARN ABOUT WHICH SUBSEGMENT REPRESENTS YOUR GREATEST MARKET OPPORTUNITY

Because there are so many different Asian subsegments, with different languages, holidays, cultures, and traditions, it's important that you understand your target consumer as much as possible. Are they Chinese? Vietnamese? Korean? You can find this information easily on Wikipedia or Freedemographics.com. You can drill down to even small towns and places and learn about the local Asian population. This is important because holidays differ, and therefore, local marketing opportunities, such as festivals and fairs, can differ dramatically.

STEP 3: EXPLORE ASIAN MEDIA OPTIONS

Once you've determined that there is a viable market opportunity with Asian consumers, educate yourself about local Asian media options. In Dallas, for example, there is a large Vietnamese population and a weekly newspaper called "But Viet" serves the Vietnamese community. This paper enjoys a strong, stable weekly readership because not only is it in Vietnamese, it covers news and information from Vietnam that are of interest to its readers. Because it's a small newspaper, advertising is relatively inexpensive and advertisers get results when they advertise in it.

STEP 4: MAKE SURE YOU USE QUALIFIED TRANSLATION SERVICES, IF NECESSARY

If you are creating a marketing message in another language, it's always important to make sure that the translation is accurate, appropriate, and meaningful. This is especially important if you don't read Asian language characters. Unlike many languages with alphabets, written Asian languages use characters. Therefore, unless you know how to read the characters, you're not going to be able to "proofread" your message. You will need to rely on a translation service or media outlet to do this for you. Most Asian media offer this service at no charge. They know that companies and brands that typically advertise in English are not going to be equipped to develop a message in an Asian language. So they provide this service free of charge. Take advantage of this service and let the media outlet do the work on this for you.

What if you're not using a media outlet such as a newspaper or radio station? Suppose those options are simply too cost-prohibitive and what you want to do is create some flyers that are targeted to Asians in your community. What then? In this case, develop your message in your primary language (for example, English) and then hire a *certified* translation company to adapt, or transcreate, the message. It's very important that you use a translation service that certifies their work; what they are essentially guaranteeing is that your message will be error free. While mistakes can happen anytime, with any company, a certified translation service will stand behind their work and make restitution if there is a problem that arises from the translation they provided. You can imagine how important certified translations are to certain businesses: anything legal, technical, or financial needs to be precise and 100 percent accurate—there is no room for "interpretation" of an insurance policy application, for example. You may pay a little more to use a certified translation service, but it's well worth the peace of mind you'll enjoy.

An additional benefit to having an accurate and meaningful translation: better brand image for you. I will never forget shopping in Peru and looking at expensive leather handbags in Lima. At one upscale, exclusive shop, the merchandise was gorgeous and beautifully displayed, the store itself was chic, the sales people were elegantly dressed, but a handmade sign by a few of the handbags read, in English: "Cheap Purse Here!" To me, it was clear what the store owner was trying to do: communicate that the handbags on sale were in a certain area of the store. But what the sign actually communicated was that the "lesser quality (cheap, meaning inferior) handbags were over here. Furthermore, the sign used "purse" (singular) rather than "purses" or "handbags" (plural). The entire effect of the poorly made sign diminished the store and its merchandise in my eyes. I am certain that the store had associates who spoke English, but I'm willing to bet that they were not perfectly fluent in English. That's why the sign had all the basic information on it, but it had no finesse. It screamed "cheesy" rather than elegant.

This leads me to another key recommendation: use a translation service rather than a friend, family member, or associate who speaks the language you want to market in. The reason for this is, just because someone can verbally speak a language, it doesn't mean they are qualified to adapt a message meaningfully in that language. Take English, for example. You probably know hundreds, if not thousands, of people who speak English. Now think about how many of those you feel are qualified to develop an ad. How many of them can really write well? Spell perfectly? Create a grammatically correct message, 100 percent of the time? Probably very few. That's because being verbally fluent in a language is not the same skill as being able to write in that language and write *well*. You don't want "cheap purse here"—you want "Designer handbags—reduced. Special prices in limited quantities," or something to that effect. So even if your neighbor speaks Chinese or one of your associates speaks and reads Japanese, resist the urge to save money by having them assist you. Hire the professional help you need. It's worth it. And remember—almost all translation companies will give you a free estimate of approximately how much it will cost to translate or transcreate/adapt your message. So you'll know upfront what the cost will be and there should be no surprises.

Note: English is the unifying language for Asian Indians. Native languages are still dominant among Chinese, Korean, and Vietnamese Americans.

STEP 5: EXPLORE ONLINE/DIGITAL MARKETING

Asians are online. Seventy-six percent of Asian-Americans use the Internet, compared to 68 percent of non-Asians. Ninety-five percent of U.S. Asians own a computer, compared to 83 percent of the total U.S. population. They are heavy users of smart phones and are likely to be influenced by bloggers and testimonials. Asians are also 12 percent more likely to do banking online and more than two thirds are actively using social networks such as Facebook, Twitter, and LinkedIn.

STEP 6: EDUCATE YOURSELF ABOUT KEY CULTURAL ASPECTS OF YOUR TARGET MARKET

For example, did you know that most Asian cultures place a great value on family closeness? Adult children in many Asian families are not necessarily expected to leave the home until they get married. Respect for elders is paramount. Managing money effectively is a valued skill and considered a virtue. Customs vary from group to group. For example, Chinese grandparents will often give their grandchild a gift of money wrapped in red paper. In Korea, on the 100th day after a child's birth, a small feast is prepared to celebrate the child. The Chinese New Year is the Lunar New Year, and the date changes every year. The Japanese New Year, however, is January 1. You can see how important it is to learn as much as possible about your Asian customer target as possible.

STEP 7: GET INVOLVED IN THE COMMUNITY

In any community that has a significant Asian population, there will be numerous ways you can become involved in the community. Fairs and festivals that celebrate Asian culture take place and it is often very affordable to have a booth or presence at such festivals. These events give you a unique opportunity to talk with your potential customers, answer questions, display your products, or share information about your services and your competitive strengths over your competitors.

"Community" doesn't have to be local. MetLife, one of the United States' most established insurance companies, has been marketing to Asian-Americans for more than 20 years. It recently sponsored a nationwide spelling bee competition—a clever way to stay connected to an important customer segment: South Asians.

Many cities and towns also have a thriving, active Asian Chamber of Commerce. If your community has an Asian Chamber of Commerce, look into joining it—you'll meet Asian business people who can be very helpful and influential as you develop targeted Asian marketing plans. You'll find that people are almost always flattered and impressed when you show sincere interest in them. They'll welcome you as a member, help you make valuable connections, perhaps even serve as a "sounding board" to bounce ideas off of.

If you become involved in the Asian community, you will find that it's a worthwhile investment that will help your business grow, now and in the future.

The U.S. Asian population is a terrific consumer segment. High income, high education, tech-savvy consumers are those that virtually every brand and company wants. Educate yourself about your market, explore local opportunities and get involved. You'll find that it will pay off.

PART THREE ➤➤
Other Important Market Segments

CHAPTER FOURTEEN ➤➤
Political Views

I recently came across an interesting article called "10 Great Retirement Spots for Democrats and Republicans." I thought to myself, "Now, *that's* a new twist on things!" Selling a retirement location based on political ideology! Who'd have thought of that? Retirement communities and articles touting cities as great places to retire usually focus on weather, cost of living, health care facilities, crime, quality of life, and so on. But when you think about it, it makes sense that people would want to live among others who share their views, their values and their way of life. And let's face it: by the time you've reached retirement, you're probably pretty certain of your views on social and political issues. You're probably not that likely to change. So taking this tactic to selling a city, a community, a housing development—it's brilliant!

Do people really buy products or services based on their political beliefs? Sure they do—and they always have. You may not have thought of it on that level, but if you buy fair-trade coffee—coffee that is purchased and distributed by companies that agree to pay the growers and farmers a fair wage—you're making a social, economic, and political statement just as much as you're making a coffee purchase. If you choose to purchase organic, free-range chicken, you're "voting with your wallet" and expressing your support on animal welfare issues.

The same is true of avoiding products based on ideology. That's what boycotts are—the refusal to purchase a company's products or services as a means to protest the way the company does business. Increasingly, because consumers are so sophisticated today and so connected and well informed, marketers must pay attention to the political arena in which products are viewed.

This is a relatively new phenomenon for marketing and it has a name: "political consumerism." Political consumerism means that we, as consumers, don't choose to buy products or services simply based on our needs. It used to be that people made purchase decisions based on several key criteria: price, value, quality, durability, reliability and availability. Today, in addition to those considerations, others are also factored into a purchase decision. Social, economic, and political issues such as a company's labor policies, commitment to the environment and being "green," community support and activism, charitable contributions, and even the political contributions made by CEOs are all reasons why consumers today buy, or don't buy, products.

It's not a fad. *Time* magazine conducted a poll among consumers and found that nearly 40 percent said they purchased a product because they liked *the social or political values of the company that produced it*. The magazine called this trend "a new kind of social contract among consumers, business and government." You can see the growth of this trend in the financial market, too: there are SRI mutual funds. "SRI funds" are "socially responsible investment" mutual funds, which generally avoid buying shares of companies that profit from such things as tobacco, oil, or child labor. SRI funds have grown from 55 in 1995 to more than 260 today. In fact, SRI funds now manage approximately 11 percent of all the money invested in U.S. financial markets.

So how do you market to people based on their political beliefs? Carefully! It's not about, "I'd like to market this deodorant to conservatives" or "This cake mix would really appeal to liberals." The opportunity lies in whether your consumer cares about the way your company or brand does business. If they do, you can incorporate some of your business philosophies into your marketing.

For example, The Gap, a well-known apparel store, developed sourcing guidelines for its suppliers and also developed a code of conduct for them. Since 2004, The Gap has been publishing information about the factories it uses and the ones it has stopped doing business with.

Timberland, maker of rugged shoes and outdoor apparel, now prints a detailed label for its shoes, noting on each pair the company's material and energy usage (see Figure 14.1).

Walmart, the world's largest retailer, now requires its suppliers to reduce packaging to protect the environment. Walmart is also giving

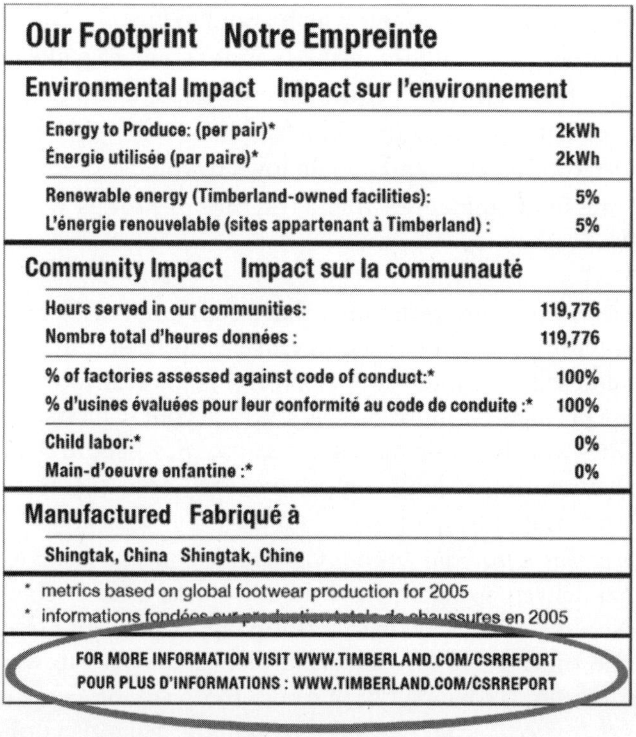

Our Footprint   Notre Empreinte

Environmental Impact   Impact sur l'environnement

Energy to Produce: (per pair)*	2kWh
Énergie utilisée (par paire)*	2kWh
Renewable energy (Timberland-owned facilities):	5%
L'énergie renouvelable (sites appartenant à Timberland) :	5%

Community Impact   Impact sur la communauté

Hours served in our communities:	119,776
Nombre total d'heures données :	119,776
% of factories assessed against code of conduct:*	100%
% d'usines évaluées pour leur conformité au code de conduite :*	100%
Child labor:*	0%
Main-d'oeuvre enfantine :*	0%

Manufactured   Fabriqué à

Shingtak, China Shingtak, Chine

* metrics based on global footwear production for 2005
* informations fondées sur production totale de chaussures en 2005

FOR MORE INFORMATION VISIT WWW.TIMBERLAND.COM/CSRREPORT
POUR PLUS D'INFORMATIONS : WWW.TIMBERLAND.COM/CSRREPORT

FIGURE 14.1   Timberland label

more shelf space and better placement to energy-efficient light bulbs in its stores, trying to entice customers to purchase them.

Mars and Cadbury have revealed plans to increase the amount of cocoa they harvest and purchase from sustainable sources. Bugaboo, maker of high-end strollers, contributes 1 percent of its revenue to the Global Fund that helps AIDS efforts in Africa. That's 1 percent of their *revenue*, not their profits.

All of these examples are part of what's now called "CSR—corporate social responsibility." Companies don't have to be socially responsible, but those that are have yet another bullet in their marketing arsenal. Let's say I intend to buy a pair of athletic shoes. It's a very competitive market and many of the shoe choices seem similar to me in quality and price. But then I learn that one company has a corporate policy of funding scholarships for kids in need. That appeals to me. If the shoe is a quality product *and* I can feel good about the company because it helps kids go to college, that's going to tip the purchase decision for me about which brand to buy.

Now, corporate social responsibility is not going to make up for an inferior product. But smart, educated consumers who become aware of what your philosophies are and what you stand for are more likely to consider your product and remain loyal to you.

Here are some guidelines for marketing to groups with various political beliefs:

- *Be sincere.* If you are promoting that your company or brand is affiliated with any form of ideology, it has to be sincere. Starbucks roasts and sells fair trade coffee. Chick-fil-A, a fast-food chain specializing in chicken sandwiches, is a very devout, Christian corporation. They are closed on Sundays because they believe that Sunday is a day of rest. They don't compromise their principles just to make more money by staying open on Sundays.

- *Be consistent with your brand.* Go Green Couriers is a courier service that delivers using only hybrid and emission-free vehicles in its fleet. You'd expect that from a company called "Go Green." But they also office remotely, allowing their employees to work from home, thereby reducing the carbon footprint of *everyone who works there because no one has to commute*. They also utilize a paperless ordering system. Everything is done online. And on top of that, every year on Earth Day, they offer free deliveries.

- *Don't let your philosophies get in the way of making your product or service the best it can be.* Everyone wants to do business with a company that shares our values and is a good "corporate citizen." But no matter how socially conscious your company is, you are first and foremost selling a product or service. That product or service should be the best it can be and the political or social ideology should only add to the consumer's enjoyment of doing business with you. It won't be enough to simply be "the good guy." You've got to be "the good product *and* the good guy." Jeff Swartz, CEO of Timberland, stated, "The vast majority of our consumers buy Timberland products because the shoe fits . . . not because we maintain a measurably higher standard of human-rights practice."

CHAPTER FIFTEEN ➤➤
Sexuality

Gay, Lesbian, Bisexual, and Transgendered

Two of my friends bought a house together not long ago. It was their first house, and they were really excited about it. Buying your first house is thrilling—and terrifying. There's a lot to know and it's a big step. So they were both a little stressed out about it. They're very meticulous, organized people and they did their homework on all the "ins and outs" of buying a home.

When they shopped for mortgages, however, they were disappointed to find that, instead of the mortgage brokers making things easier for them, the brokers actually added to the stress of the situation. In meeting after meeting with various brokers and lenders, they found that aspect of the process to be very difficult. Why? Because my friends are gay. Their very presence, sitting in a bank across from a loan officer or across the desk from a broker, made these loan executives uncomfortable. Dave stated to me, "You could tell these guys had no experience with a gay couple trying to get a mortgage. They were so nervous—couldn't even look us in the eye—either one of us! Why would I want to do business with someone who can't even look me in the eye?"

Dave and Don ended up using a mortgage broker from the Gay Mortgage Directory.

The interesting thing was, the broker they used was not gay! They found a local broker through the directory and through the course of several conversations with him, Dave and Don learned that the broker was not gay. They were intrigued by this and asked him, "So why do you advertise and market yourself in the Gay Mortgage Directory if you're not gay yourself?" The broker replied, "Because years ago, I realized that a lot of people in my business completely ignore the gay and lesbian market and I figured that, in addition to my straight customers, I could get a lot of gay and lesbian customers, too. No one was really going after this market. Now I am, and 30 percent of my business is gay and lesbian couples."

The mortgage broker wasn't gay. He was *gay-friendly*. And he was really smart. He saw a market opportunity and he grabbed it. The gay, lesbian, bisexual, and transgender market (hereafter referred to as GLBT) is lucrative and very loyal. For many businesses, it makes sense to target these consumers. Here are some key reasons why marketers are interested in this segment. GLBT consumers are:

1. *Affluent.* The average annual income for a gay/lesbian household is 20 percent higher than in a heterosexual household. Additionally, many gay and lesbian couples do not have children, thereby increasing their discretionary income.
2. *Educated.* Eighty-three percent of gays and lesbians have either attended or graduated from college.
3. *Loyal.* Approximately 89 percent of gays and lesbians say they are highly likely to seek out brands that advertise to them.

The GLBT community is very responsive to the brands, companies, and products that market to them. Why? Because many advertisers have, for the most part, shied away from directly targeting the

GLBT community for fear of a "backlash" among other customers who don't accept homosexuals. With other customer segments, such as minorities or various religious groups, it would be considered racist or incredibly intolerant of diversity to exclude those customer segments in marketing messages. But there are those who feel that being lesbian or gay is a choice, and therefore, believe that GLBT consumers are not a "true" diversity target. As a marketing professional, I know that the GLBT market is lucrative and loyal, and I have seen companies flourish by "putting the welcome mat out" for the GLBT community.

One of the most notable case studies for GLBT marketing is Subaru. In the 1990s, Subaru was struggling in the United States and was perilously close to going out of business. The marketing team at Subaru identified a number of characteristics of their owner base (such as occupation, age, race/ethnicity, active outdoor lifestyles, etc.) and one of their findings was that a significant percentage of their owners were lesbian or gay. Subaru carved out a portion of their marketing budget and allocated it specifically to the GLBT community. They hired a GLBT ad agency to guide them and create relevant messaging. They took a 360-degree approach, sponsoring major GLBT events and displaying their vehicles at those events. The Subaru personnel who staffed the events, answering questions about the vehicles and explaining features and benefits, were given sensitivity and diversity training to make sure that the company was, indeed, gay-friendly in its customer communications. But perhaps one of the most notable things that Subaru did was offer domestic partnership benefits to its employees. At the time, this was groundbreaking. No other automobile manufacturer in the United States offered domestic partnership benefits then. Considering that Subaru was (and still is) tiny compared to General Motors, Ford, and Toyota, the fact that they were first to offer this employee benefit was truly revolutionary. Today, virtually all the major automotive companies offer domestic partnership benefits, but Subaru was the first and word spread through the GLBT community that Subaru was "authentic." They weren't just making clever ads and placing them in gay publications. They were supporting the GLBT community and backing that support up with corporate diversity initiatives that held real meaning.

This is an important lesson if you want to market effectively to the GLBT community. You've got to be gay-friendly. Most people know someone who is gay, so insensitive messaging or business practices will be ineffective, if not outright damaging. You don't have to be gay or lesbian to create a great GLBT targeted ad. You've just got to be sensitive to the needs of the GLBT community and respectful of their triumphs and struggles.

Here's an example of demonstrating sensitivity to the GLBT community. The travel and tourism industry was one of the first to recognize the enormous potential of lesbians and gays. Not only do many gay and lesbian couples have high discretionary income, but travel is one of the key categories that they spend that discretionary income on. It makes sense: many couples can't be openly "out" at home or at work or in their communities. But the one place you really ought to be able to relax and be yourself is when you're on vacation, right? There is a lot of GLBT-targeted tourism, but the ad for Key West seen in Figure 15.1 is one of my favorites, because it gets across several important, relevant messages:

- The headline "Come as You Are" speaks to the casual, laid-back nature of Key West.
- The copy in the ad expands on that, promoting "live and let live." In other words, you can be yourself and I can be myself and we'll respect each other's rights to live as we choose and be who we are.
- The reference to "One Human Family" and "everyone is welcome" is inclusive. Although the ad is clearly aimed at the GLBT community, it doesn't exclude heterosexuals. It communicates that straight people are welcome as well. It does an outstanding job of communicating that Key West is a tolerant community and a mellow, laid-back one at that. Sounds like a great place to go for a vacation!

What makes this ad sensitive to the GLBT community is that it communicates that, although you may or may not be able to walk down the street holding hands with your partner back at home, you can certainly do so in Key West. With just a few words, the message tells the reader to "come to Key West, relax, you're among friends." Key West also further targeted gay men and lesbians separately, with different ads.

FIGURE 15.1   Key West Advertisement

Another great example of GLBT marketing, this time celebrating triumphs, is Bella Pictures, of San Francisco, California. Bella Pictures is a professional photography firm specializing in wedding photography and video. Their work is exceptional—tasteful, timeless, and elegant. Their wedding portraits truly capture the joy and magic of the couple's special day. In California, when gay and lesbian couples were granted the right to legally wed, Bella Pictures knew this was a landmark moment and that many GLBT couples had been waiting for this day for decades. The right to legally marry is a big deal for GLBT couples and their loved ones. It's recognition, validation, and civil liberties, all rolled into one.

FIGURE 15.2   Bella Pictures Advertisement

Bella Pictures was a "straight" wedding photography company looking to celebrate the first GLBT weddings . . . and also market themselves as GLBT-friendly to an emerging market of same-sex couples about to get married. They perfectly captured the excitement and historic significance of this day with their ad, "Coming out to City Hall?"(see Figure 15.2). The copy in the ad read, "Bella Pictures will be there taking FREE wedding photos on Day One!" This ad impressed me for several reasons:

1. The ad featured real people, not models. The couple is attractive, but relatable. Their embrace, big smiles, matching tuxedos, and the prominence of the wedding ring clearly communicate that this is their Big Day.

2. The elaborate doors of City Hall behind them show what a grand institution this city government building represents. These doors have always been closed to GLBT couples until now. But in this ad, the doors to City Hall are open—to everyone.

3. The headline – "Coming out to City Hall?" is clever. It's a play on "coming out," of course, but it's tasteful, not stereotypical. The headline conveys, "This is what you've been waiting for." It says, "Don't wait! Don't miss this opportunity!" It's far more clever—and interesting—than saying, "Getting married?"

4. Finally, the element that I love most about this ad is the reference to Day One. No one in the GLBT community would need to have that explained to them. This day was so historic, so emotional, so long overdue, and Bella Pictures wanted to be there to celebrate *weddings*—which is what they do—with all the couples who were going to marry on that day.

5. The company took the wedding photos for free. Sure, they could have charged for them, and plenty of couples would have paid handsomely for the wedding portraits, but it's so much more authentic, so much more genuine, to acknowledge and celebrate Day One with free wedding portraits. And celebrating is exactly what was happening that day. What better way to truly support the GLBT community than to honor that day with free photography?

And speaking of support, Stuart Gaffney, one of the grooms in the Bella Pictures ad, had this to say about marketing to gays and lesbians:

> Bella Pictures did a photo shoot with us for the ad, and gave us the rights to the photos—the only stipulation was that we credit them if we used the photos elsewhere. We've had occasion to use the photos numerous times—from documentary films to magazine spreads—thus giving credit and further publicity to the wedding photographer. I would recommend this company to this day to any friends—straight or gay—planning a wedding.

That's the kind of reference and loyalty most companies would love to have.

Support of any diverse target segment should go beyond advertising. Most GLBT consumers say that the ads from companies, big and small, that make a difference with them are those that are related to supporting community events and institutions. For example, a friend told me about seeing an ad for AT&T in the schedule for an upcoming GLBT film festival. She noted that AT&T was the festival's "grand sponsor." Her comment was, "The fact that AT&T is giving significant funding to a community event I value is more important to me than whether AT&T has a gay ad in mainstream media."

If you want to effectively target the GLBT community, one of the best things you can do to demonstrate that you value the community is to "start at home," by ensuring that your business is gay-friendly. This means having nondiscrimination policies in the workplace, domestic partner or same-sex spousal insurance for employees, and other tangible benefits that show you're not just good at marketing, but you're also a good place to work. Workplace rankings provided by several GLBT organizations are followed closely by many in the community.

Another key thing to keep in mind when marketing to the GLBT community is to avoid stereotypes. Melissa Timmerman, a manager at one of the largest and most successful gay clubs in Dallas, states, "There are so many ads that portray gays and lesbians as promiscuous and sex-crazy. That's insulting. And not very realistic. You don't have to create a sexy ad to reach me. Just tell me about your product or service, make it relevant to me, and show me that you value me as a customer." Her sentiments are echoed by many in the GLBT community. Here are two ads that were discussed during a recent panel discussion on GLBT marketing. The panel of gay men and women unanimously agreed that the BMW ad, although clever, was offensive and insulting (see Figure 15.3). "When the top's away, the car will play" has a double meaning in this example. "Tops and bottoms" are slang for gay sex positions. By using these terms, BMW is clearly targeting the gay community. But the offensive part is the insinuation that "when one partner is away, the other will play." "It's as if they think no one who's gay can be faithful or committed to another person, and that's insulting." said one panelist. Compare that with the ad for Wells Fargo (see Figure 15.4), featuring two women who are clearly partnered and planning their future together. The Wells Fargo ad demonstrates respect and treats the topic—combined finances—very seriously.

Another example of a well-done ad is this one for Embassy Suites (see Figure 15.5). The headline and copy don't scream, "Hey gays and lesbians! Stay at this hotel!," but the photo clearly shows that the travelers are both men. It's tasteful and targeted. Timmerman states, "My sexuality does not define me. There's more to me than just my sexual preference." Tim Bennett, a marketing

FIGURE 15.3   BMW Advertisement

consultant who specializes in niche marketing, including GLBT marketing, agrees. "An ad like this is appealing because it gives good reasons to choose Embassy Suites, like value and proximity to the beach, but it's also demonstrating that the company truly cares about the gay community. They're a sponsor of the Gay Pride festival, and the image in the ad is relevant."

Here are some other Do's and Don'ts for marketing effectively to the GLBT community, courtesy of the GLAAD Advertising Media Program Best Practices:

When two accounts become one

Sharing expenses is a big step and Wells Fargo will help you take it. Together we'll
navigate the maze of your personal finances and find solutions tailored to both of your
needs. Wells Fargo has a wide range of accounts and services that help you achieve your
financial goals. From flexible checking and savings accounts, loan offerings to premier
investment management services, we'll work with you to help you save, plan and prepare
for the future. Talk to a Wells Fargo banker today and take your big step with confidence.

wellsfargo.com/lgbt

Together we'll go far

© 2009 Wells Fargo Bank, N.A.
All rights reserved. Member FDIC. (120570_12099)

FIGURE 15.4   Wells Fargo Advertisement

FIGURE 15.5   Embassy Suites Hotel Advertisement

DO

- Do avoid using clichés and alienating GLBT stereotypes and homophobia.
- Do become aware of the differences between cross-dressers/transvestites, transsexuals, male-to-females, female-to-males, androgyny, and female impersonator/drag queens.

- Do recognize that GLBT people come from all races, ages, ethnicities, nationalities, incomes, political and religious affiliations, professions, physical abilities, and gender expressions, and whenever possible, incorporate such diversity into their representations. One size does not fit all.
- Do understand that a few consumers will shun your brand for being GLBT-friendly.
- Do recognize that GLBT people already are your customers
- Do understand it is important to test GLBT-themed ads, including those emphasizing masculine or feminine characteristics, with GLBT perspectives and in focus groups.

DON'T

- Don't engage social conservatives in debate regarding GLBT issues, when criticized; business and respect for faith are separate issues.
- Don't waffle, modify, or withdraw GLBT-friendly campaigns. Be consistent and principled.
- Don't hyperventilate about backlash and boycott threats. Experience shows that most provocation is politically motivated and intended for near-term shock and awe. Companies find that these episodes almost always blow over quickly.
- Don't use GLBT stereotypes, themes, or people as a device to elicit shock, humor, or titillation.
- Don't use horrified or violent revulsion to references of homosexuality or transgender people.
- Don't label or degrade gay men or lesbians as sexual predators.
- Don't use sexuality in a degrading way to characterize same-sex affection and intimacy—or associate sexual practices with gays and lesbians differently than with heterosexuals.
- Don't characterize transgender people as deceptive, scary, or freakish.
- Don't characterize bisexuals as cheaters.

The GLBT market can be a terrific new opportunity for your business. It doesn't matter if you're gay or straight. What matters is sincerely recognizing the business potential and taking steps, internally and externally, to put the welcome mat out for this lucrative and loyal customer segment.

CHAPTER SIXTEEN ▶▶
Hobbies and Special Interests

Have you heard of Mensa International? Mensa is the "high IQ society," a group of people all over the world who have attained a score within the upper 2 percent of the general population on intelligence. It's a global organization and, as you might imagine, those who are Mensa members share much more than simply a higher IQ than average. They also share a love of knowledge and intellectual exchange. They appreciate and enjoy intellectual challenges. They like to push themselves intellectually. So let's say you have a company that makes puzzles and games, and up until now, you've always focused on kids and young adults. You want to expand your business, and you decide to create a new product line: extremely challenging puzzles and games designed to stretch the "mind muscles" of the player. Targeting a group like Mensa members would make perfect sense.

In previous chapters, we've addressed targeting certain groups by race, ethnicity, gender, age, and even nativity. But finding new customers through their hobbies or interests can open doors for your business as well. And, as in the case of Mensa members, you may find that the only common link among a group who share a hobby is the *hobby*. Mensa members are all over the world. They are men and women, young and old, of every race, ethnicity, income, and education level you can imagine. But there is a strong common platform that they share, and that is their minds and the way their minds work.

You can grow your business by expanding into hobbies and special interests to find new customers. Major companies do this all the time. For example, Starbucks started off as a coffeehouse. Their locations served coffee and coffee drinks and, of course, tea as well. But down the road, they realized that there are many people who don't drink coffee or tea, and therefore would be unlikely to visit a Starbucks location. So they started serving chocolate. Not just hot chocolate to drink, but also chocolate candies and gourmet nuts. They began marketing their chocolate selections online on web sites devoted to chocolate, and placed ads in "foodie" magazines and articles. By doing so, they brought in more customers to the stores and also expanded their brand beyond just coffee. Today, Starbucks sells not only coffee, tea, and chocolate, but premium ice cream, too (see Figures 16.1 and 16.2).

FIGURE 16.1   Starbucks Ice Cream

FIGURE 16.2   Starbucks Chocolate

This leads me to another key strategy when targeting people who share hobbies or common interests: marketing affiliated (linked) products to a new group based on certain assumptions. In the case of Starbucks, they knew that people who enjoy—and are willing to pay for—premium coffee are also likely to enjoy premium chocolate. And premium ice cream. In other words, these customers like the best-tasting food and drinks, and they are willing to pay the premium price to have them.

Another example of affiliated product marketing would be targeting cigar smokers to sell wine or brandy. There are two types of cigar smokers: those who puff on a regular basis and those who enjoy an occasional cigar. Of those who enjoy the occasional cigar, many times the "occasion" is centered around either a celebration or a fine meal. The "cigar after dinner" can be part of the ritual of a good meal. So it follows that if you are the maker of wine, a great affiliated target customer base is cigar smokers. Chances are, those who enjoy a good cigar after a meal also enjoy a glass of fine wine or a great brandy.

A friend of mine owns a family vineyard. They market their wines to cigar smokers and to leisure travelers. They place ads in publications focused on cigar smoking, they find local upscale smoke shops and form relationships with the owners or managers and place information about their wines there, and even offer to do wine tastings. They also advertise in travel publications because they know that people who can afford to travel for leisure can also afford to eat out and drink wine.

Another example of affiliated product marketing is hunting and fly-fishing. For most game, in most parts of the world, there is a very specific time of the year that is designated as hunting season. Therefore, hunters are confined to just a few weeks or months of the year in which to pursue their passion. If I owned a fly-fishing store, or was the maker of fly-fishing gear, I'd try marketing the experience of fly-fishing to hunting enthusiasts. Why? Because both types of people tend to love the outdoors and being in the wilderness, and they also have a love of adventure. They love the challenge of matching their wits and their skill against nature. Also, the two sports have complementary seasons. Hunting is usually an autumn and winter activity, while fly-fishing is typically spring and summer. Therefore, the customer who loves to hunt may have some leisure time on his hands in the summer and would perhaps enjoy trying a new experience. And, finally, both of these sports can be expensive. The needed gear and equipment alone can cost hundreds, if not thousands, of dollars. So if I owned a fly-fishing store, hunters would make a good potential prospect for me because I already know that they can afford the sport and are willing to pay good money to do so. If they can afford hunting, they can probably afford fly-fishing.

Here are some other examples of affiliated activities products or consumers:

- Wine and cheese or gourmet cooking
- Film lovers, art lovers, and music lovers
- Museum lovers and theater lovers
- Video gamers and tech products
- Fashion and beauty products
- Sports and nutrition
- Home and garden

So how do you reach members of a group that have a particular hobby or interest? Here are seven primary ways:

1. Direct marketing
2. Special interest magazines or web sites
3. Editorial contributions
4. Venue marketing
5. Niche marketing (relationship marketing)
6. Association marketing
7. Connectors

DIRECT MARKETING

Direct marketing means reaching your target prospect directly. It usually means reaching them through targeted mailings or e-mails or targeted online efforts, such as placing "cookies" on web sites so that you can track visitors to a site and then redirect them to another site. You can buy mailing lists and e-mail lists for just about every conceivable type of customer group there is. Direct marketing can also include television advertising. For example, let's say you manufacture and market a cleaning product that is designed for major, heavy-duty cleaning. It's best used on plaster and brick. You decide to create a television commercial with a strong "call to action," such as "Order online now and get two for the price of one" or "Call 1-888-XXX-XXXX and get two for the price of one." Then you run that commercial during a program that focuses on how to fix up an old house. That would be an example of direct marketing because only those people who are interested in fixing up an old house are likely to be watching the show. And they are the ones who would be most likely to need and want your product. Direct marketing can be costly but highly effective because you're truly "narrowcasting." You're reaching only those people who are most likely to be interested in your product or service.

SPECIAL INTEREST MAGAZINES OR WEB SITES

This is a highly effective way of reaching those who share a hobby or special interest because there's no waste—the only people you'll reach are those you want to reach. There are special interest publications and web sites for everything—no hobby or area of interest is too small or obscure. Let's say you want to reach stamp collectors, coin collectors, or doll collectors. There are hundreds of sites devoted to the collector's passion as well as blogs and numerous organizations. Placing an ad in a specialized publication or on a web site can really boost your business because 100 percent of the readership is your target.

EDITORIAL CONTRIBUTIONS

If you have a small marketing budget, or *no* marketing budget, one way to get valuable exposure with special interest groups is to submit an article to the main specialty publications that serve that group. Publications are always looking for good content, and they are usually open to accepting articles from "guest contributors," especially if the article is noncommercial. By that, I mean that you shouldn't try to pass off a "commercial" or ad for your product or service as an editorial article. But what you can do is offer professional advice or a point of view that would be relevant to readers. In the preceding example for the home cleaning product, you could write an article on "Refreshing the Look of Your Home for Less than $300." The article could talk about how the simple, thorough cleaning of a brick exterior can make a home look 10 years newer. The article could tell readers about the critical steps they need to take to wash the brick surface properly and perhaps offer some do's and don'ts. At the end of the article, your name can include your company name or the name of your product and some contact information. For example, *"John Smith is the owner of Smith's Industrial-Strength Cleaning Products, a line of heavy-duty products for cleaning home exteriors. The company web site is www.xxxxxxxx.com."*

By contributing an article that guides readers to a solution or offers help for a problem, you are positioning yourself as an expert. Most specialty publications will eagerly welcome such articles. Contact the editor of the publication, introduce yourself, and tell them what you have in mind and ask if they accept articles from outside contributors. Just remember to make the article noncommercial.

VENUE MARKETING

Venue marketing is about being where your customers and prospects are. Stadium advertising and sponsorships fall into this category. In most major cities around the world, stadiums and arenas have been corporately named and other sponsors place ads on the inside of the arena. For some products, this makes great sense. Budweiser beer, for example, definitely wants to have sponsorships and ads in sporting and concert stadiums, since sports and music and drinking beer go hand-in-hand.

But there are less expensive ways to use venue marketing to reach a special interest group. Let's say you're a massage therapist and you're trying to build your practice with a steady clientele. You know that people who need massages are often people who pull muscles either at work or by playing a sport. So you offer to do free "chair massages" at a local 10K or half-marathon race. You give the runners a complimentary 10-minute back massage on site and offer them a special coupon with a discount for a follow-up, full hour massage. The next weekend, you do the same at a local construction and contracting expo.

Suppose you make your own jewelry from all natural materials, and you need additional exposure to sell more of your merchandise. Find a local event that is focused on a compatible topic, such as natural food or art festivals featuring local artists or holistic arts, and rent a booth or table to display your wares.

Many manufacturers of products for the outdoors use this method to expose their highest-potential customers to their products at very little costs. I have seen such companies spend the day at a ski resort, passing out samples of hand warmers, lip balm, and other cold-weather related products. For just the cost of the labor and some samples, they have the ability to be right where their best prospects are, get their products into the hands of the user, answer questions, and be part of the experience. All because they were smart enough to find the right venue and participate in it in a meaningful way.

NICHE MARKETING (RELATIONSHIP MARKETING)

Niche marketing, also known as relationship marketing, is a great way to reach potential customers with a shared interest or lifestyle. The "niche" can be almost anything: it can be work, religion, education, lifestyle, politics, sports, and so on. By focusing on a niche, you can tailor your message to the specific needs or wants of a group.

Mark Nash, a top real estate executive with Coldwell Banker, recommends niche marketing to expand business. He uses the example of a realtor who is also an avid mountain biker and outlines specific recommendations on how the realtor can use that niche (mountain biking) to grow his or her business. It works like this:

First, you join the International Mountain Bicycling Association and develop relationships with other bikers. Over time, you'll develop a number of relationships that result in what Nash calls "walking, talking billboards for your real estate business." These are your new friends that you've made through the group, and they know what you do for a living, so they're happy to refer you to anyone they come across who may need your services.

Next, let's say after a year of attending meetings and events of fellow mountain bikers, you decide to place an ad in the program book of the group's annual convention, letting attendees know that if they or family members are considering a move to your community, they should call a fellow bicycling enthusiast for their home search.

But wait—there's more! At one of the local meetings you attend, a new member is introduced. She has her own law firm in a nearby community and handles real estate transactions. You meet her and offer to refer clients to her practice. After a while, you're both referring clients to each other. Eventually, the lawyer introduces you to a mortgage broker, and the three of you actively refer clients to each other. Down the line, you decide to start a web site for mountain bikers that features the businesses of members, as well as regional sports news. You can have your own real estate pages on the web site, and you're fully working this niche of mountain biking to grow your business.

To be effective with niche marketing, you must have a sincere interest in your niche, or the members of the group will see through purely monetary motives. Nash states that "giving back to the niche is also a critical part of successfully serving a niche." In this example, the realtor created a web site for *all* the businesses in the mountain bike group.

ASSOCIATION MARKETING

Association marketing is not unlike niche marketing. Many of the same steps apply: becoming involved with a group or organization, forming relationships based on trust, and building on those relationships over time. The difference is that niche marketing targets people within a group, whereas association marketing targets the organization itself. Association marketing can be a powerful way to reach special interest groups because:

- Prospects are accessible through regular meetings and conventions.
- If you are part of the association, you have an inherent credibility factor. You're "one of them," not just a vendor trying to sell something.
- You can learn a tremendous amount about your fellow members through association correspondence.

The first step in association marketing is to identify those organizations that fit your product or service well. Contact the association and ask for a meeting with an influential member, such as an officer or board member. Most associations have a membership director, and they are usually very eager to meet with potential new members. When making the appointment, clearly state that it is a fact-finding get-together on how you might benefit the association membership, and that you're not trying to sell anything. (Associations are typically bombarded with people and companies trying to gain access to them and their members, so they are understandably very protective of their members and reluctant to talk to those they consider just trying to make a sale.)

The purpose of your meeting is to introduce yourself as a resource and to learn how you can cultivate a mutually beneficial relationship. You'll want to learn as much as you can about the association and how it works to see if it's a good match for you. Joining associations can be costly—you'll have to pay a membership fee—so make sure the ones you target are a fit.

Larry Cox, an insurance executive who specializes in association marketing, offers these key questions to ask when meeting with an association executive:

- How can I best be accepted as a resource with your members?
- What's the best way to approach your members? What's the worst way?
- When does the association meet? Where?
- What kinds of speakers do you use to educate members? Who arranges the program?
- In what other ways do you communicate? (Magazine, newsletter, e-mail, etc.)
- When is the best time to call someone in your profession/industry/club/association?

Cox also advises that you assure the association leader that you will use his or her name only to open doors, not as an endorsement (until permission is given).

Once you've joined an association or have been given permission to market to its members, develop a marketing plan. Your tactics might include printing a brochure, direct mailing members with a specific offer, developing a newsletter, or speaking at meetings.

Your objective is to earn a strong endorsement from the association leadership. If you are sincere, active, and focused on how you can best help the members of an association, you'll be welcomed and make many sales.

CONNECTORS

Connectors are those people who, in any given group or organization, have major influence. What they say matters to the rest of the group, and they have tremendous ability to shape opinions. In the preceding example regarding the mountain bikers, connectors for the realtor were the mortgage broker and real estate attorney. One of the best case studies I've come across regarding connectors involves the milk industry and how it was able to boost sales of milk, specifically chocolate milk.

New research shows that low-fat chocolate milk helps the body recover after exercise more effectively than sports drinks. Of course, this new research caught the attention of the milk industry in the United States. To help spread the word on this "new news" and to increase milk sales, the milk industry targeted teenagers who participate in high school sports. Teens are big milk drinkers to begin with, and those involved in

FIGURE 16.3   Milk Advertisement

school sports make a perfect target. But how to go about reaching them? The milk industry targeted high school *coaches*. Coaches are influencers. They are looked up to and they are trusted. So when coaches started telling their student athletes to drink chocolate milk after workouts, those students started telling their parents to buy chocolate milk. And milk sales grew tremendously. In this case, the coaches were *connectors;* they weren't the target prospect at all—the students were. But the coaches were powerfully connected to the students, and by reaching the coaches with a message on the benefits of chocolate milk, that message filtered down to the right target (see Figure 16.3).

Another example of connectors are "haulers"—teens who shop frequently for clothing and accessories and have tremendous style, but also tremendous ability to stretch their budgets. They pride themselves on "making hauls" and showing off how much merchandise they were able to buy and how little they spent. JCPenney recognizes these influential teens and uses them in viral Web videos to showcase new fashion finds that they got at JCPenney. The company actively courts these haulers and incentivizes them to shop at JCPenney and then post their video hauls on YouTube.

Connectors are everywhere. Every group has them. They are the people who can influence others because of their position, their stature, their network, or simply their personality. You can tap into groups of people who share a hobby or special interest by identifying the connectors within that group.

CHAPTER SEVENTEEN ▶▶
Rural versus Metro

Here's a pretty substantial way that people can be very, very different from each other: if they live in a major metropolitan area or if they live in a rural area. This type of market segmentation has nothing to do with race, ethnicity, language, age, or even hobbies and special interests. It has to do with a way of life. A culture. Values. And these things shape the way that people interact and what they want and need. Each type of community has its strengths and weaknesses.

METRO (URBAN) LIVING

Metro living means choices. Whether it's choices in food (abundant restaurants and cafes), shopping, schools, health care, cultural events, or more employment options, living in a metropolitan area offers lots of choices. It also usually means that people are more exposed to diversity, whether that means racial and ethnic diversity or people from other social, cultural, and economic groups. There are tremendous advantages to metro living and tremendous disadvantages as well: higher crime rates, traffic, pollution, noise, lack of green space, higher cost of living, and so on. People in metro areas often seem busier and less connected to one another.

RURAL LIVING

By contrast, rural areas are not crowded, and people in rural areas live in close proximity to nature. Apart from people, there is room for pets and grazing animals that help maintain equilibrium in nature. Much of the stress that results from a fast-paced life in metro areas is not a part of a peaceful and relatively slow-paced life of a rural area. People tend to know their neighbors in rural communities. And while there may be less diversity, there is usually a strong sense of community because rural living means being able to rely on your friends and neighbors.

So how does this affect marketing? Profoundly. The types of products that people want and need differ dramatically between metro and rural. In the country, a man may go to a "barber" and get a $10 haircut. In the city, he'll go to a "stylist" and pay $50. Three quarters of the pickup trucks that are sold in the United States are sold in rural areas. Chances are, you just don't need a truck if you live in downtown Manhattan. In fact, you probably don't need a vehicle at all. You probably won't find too many sushi restaurants in the country, but you will find lots of diners that offer good, simple, "country cooking" at reasonable prices. Clothing needs are vastly different from metro to rural as well. If you live in a metro area, you probably need more clothes: you'd need clothes for work, clothes for casual wear, and clothes for dressing up and going to upscale places. In the country, you'd need more functional clothes—clothes that can weather the elements outdoors or keep you warm. You probably don't need suits and ties and evening gowns.

Beyond the obvious differences between metro and rural consumers, there are more subtle ones. And these differences spill over into marketing. One of the most intriguing products that I've come across lately is shapewear for men. *Shapewear* is the modern term for *girdle*. It's a huge industry, and women buy shapewear in every conceivable type of garment.

Now, Equmen, an Australian line, has launched a line of shapewear for men. They call their line "compression garments" and sell tank tops and T-shirts that cost more than $100. Spanx and Sculptees are other major brands that have launched similar products. They're sold at upscale metropolitan department stores like Saks, Bloomingdale's and Nordstrom's—stores you'll find only in major metro areas. Men who live in metro areas are likely to buy this product because many aspects of their lives may be tied to their appearance: their social life, dating, their work environment, and more. I doubt that most men who live in rural areas would have much use for men's shapewear! Aside from the product itself (which is selling like crazy, I must add), the language that is used to market it is clearly designed to put men at ease. Many men are uncomfortable with vanity; they may feel it's not "manly" to want to look good and to pamper themselves. The ad for the Equmen T-shirt stresses that it's a "base layer" (not shapewear) and that it offers "support for your body" (see Figure 17.1). The ad also talks about looking your best on "interview days." Clearly, the target is metro men who don't mind paying more than $100 for a T-shirt to be worn under other clothes. I just can't imagine that being a priority for a man living in a rural area.

Rural marketing is just as specific. Because people who live in rural communities tend to know each other, the approach they often take with each other is direct and honest. "Plain-speaking" is one phrase, and ads targeted to rural residents reflect that. An example of that plain talk is on the web site for Rural Singles of America, an

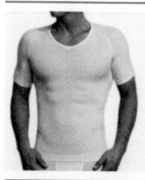

Core Precision V-Neck Undershirt

The Equmen Core Precision V-Neck Undershirt, from the Equmen Mens Collection, is an innovative base layer that actually slims and streamlines your look while offering support for your body. Made to fit tight to give optimum performance, this Equmen undershirt was designed in conjunction with physiotherapists and ergonomic specialists to improve posture, reduce back pain and provide core support. Wear the Equmen Core Precision V-Neck Undershirt under a work shirt or sweater whenever you want to be sure to look your best (for example: on interview days or your wedding day).

FIGURE 17.1   Equmen Advertisement

online dating service dedicated solely to "horse people, active farmers, and ranchers." It makes perfect sense; the wide-open spaces of rural living also means fewer people. Therefore, if you're single and living in a rural area, it may be hard to meet someone. And if you do meet someone, it may be hard for them to understand the demands of your country life. Raising horses or running a farm or ranch requires long hours and hard work. It's probably very important for single, rural people who live and work in those professions to meet others who can understand and appreciate the demands of that lifestyle.

But just as in the Equmen ad for the compression T-shirt, the choice of words matters. The web site for the Rural Singles of America invites you to browse their listings for "Country Fellas" and "Country Gals," not just "men" or "women" (see Figure 17.2a and b). That's language that is specific to rural living. It's very appropriate for the site's target prospects and what they're looking for.

FIGURE 17.2A   Rural Singles of America Advertisement

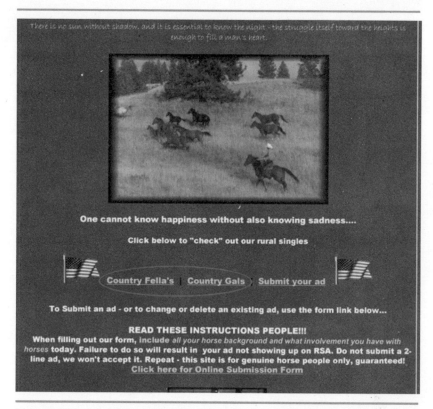

FIGURE 17.2B   Rural Singles of America Advertisement

As you think about whether your product or service should be marketed to metro or rural residents (and I think it would be pretty obvious), pay attention to even the language that you use. Make sure your marketing message communicates authenticity and reflects how people really think and speak.

CHAPTER EIGHTEEN ➤
Military versus Civilian

I can hardly think of two more different worlds than the military and civilian worlds. Everything is different: the manner in which people dress, the codes of conduct, the pressures and demands of day-to-day life, the pressure on family life—everything! Even the police and court systems are different. And the language: *commissary* instead of *supermarket,* and so on. In marketing to people not like you, the military market should not be overlooked if you have products or services that may fill a need or help ease some of the stress and pressures that military personnel and their loved ones face.

If you want to tap into the military market, there are some things you should know and consider to ensure that your efforts will be successful.

First, while all militaries around the world are different, they share some common traits, including a profile of active duty service members that looks something like this:

- Young, primarily between the ages of 18 and 34
- 85 percent male
- Technologically advanced, 95 percent are Internet enabled
- Physically fit

In the United States, about half of the active service members are married, and about half of the married couples have children. Military personnel make extremely attractive target customers for many businesses because they are 100 percent employed. Furthermore, enlisted men and women earn 40 percent more than the average high school graduate. This is due, in large part, to the fact that they receive base pay as well as many other tax-free allowances that are tied to their rank: where they're stationed, whether they live on or off the base, what type of military specialty they have, and so on. On top of that, many of their day-to-day living expenses are dramatically lower than those of civilians. Food and household goods bought in military grocery stores are priced just 5 percent higher than cost. Gasoline purchased on base costs substantially less than at gas stations off base. Food and lodging is free for those who live on base and eat in the mess hall. And, of course, health care costs are covered by the government. This profile is an ideal customer segment for many companies and products, but it's often overlooked.

Second, understand that military personnel and their families and loved ones face unique challenges. Long or frequent deployments take their toll on everyone. Military families are faced with constant moving, family separations, and pulling their kids in and out of schools every couple of years. Your products, services, and marketing efforts should support military personnel, never exploit them. Certain political and religious special interest groups, as well as financial organizations, have been known to market aggressively to the military, with less-than-transparent, truthful information. These aggressive tactics are never recommended and, over time, usually backfire anyway, causing a backlash against the entity that wanted military consumers' business in the first place.

Third, be sensitive to the feelings of service members and their loved ones. For example, in the United States, Memorial Day is a major national holiday on the last Monday in May. Memorial Day is the day when Americans remember and mourn the service men and women who have died in combat. There is no postal service that day, most banks are closed that day, and many businesses are closed as well. Because so many businesses close to observe the holiday, their workers have a three-day weekend. And because all across the United States the weather is usually quite nice at the end of May, people celebrate the holiday with friends and barbeques. Over the years, this socializing has led to less emphasis on the meaning of the holiday and more emphasis on "good times and getting together with friends for burgers and beer." In fact, when people wish each other "Happy Memorial Day," it can be a tremendous disconnect for those with loved ones in the armed forces and downright painful for those who have lost someone to war. While many people use the day to pray for troops or remember fallen service members, others are shopping at the mall and throwing backyard parties. Paul Rieckhoff, executive director of Iraq and Afghanistan Veterans of America, describes the cultural gap between military and civilian families this way: "There's a disconnect every day, but I think it's felt even more so on Memorial Day. The average American family goes to the beach or goes to a barbeque. The average military family goes to a cemetery." Be sensitive to these types of nuances. You would never want to create an ad that would run in a *military newspaper* that read, "Memorial Day savings! Fifty percent off all merchandise!" It could be viewed as tasteless, insensitive, and out of touch with your target audience.

So how do you go about reaching the military market? Here are six tips to get started:

1. *If you have a service or product that you want to market to the military, are you willing to create a special military offer?*. Many brands and services offer reduced prices or special deals to service members, and this can create initial demand and ongoing loyalty. Janice Thompson of SiteEDGE Agency, a marketing and advertising firm with experience in military marketing, advises that if you do offer a special price or deal, position it as *"thank you for your service,"* rather than promoting the savings. Military households tend to have above-average disposable incomes, so the "thank you" recognition is more meaningful than a "savings" message.

2. *Know your audience.* The military today is not the military of 20 years ago. There are more women serving, and the Armed

Forces are very Internet-savvy and tightly networked. Make sure your military marketing includes online and social media components that will produce word-of-mouth advertising and referrals (see Figure 18.1).

3. *Don't overdo the patriotic message.* You don't have to use a waving flag in every message. In fact, there are so many images of flags in military marketing, it's become a cliché.

4. *Don't make uniform mistakes.* If you choose to show someone in uniform, make sure the uniform is 100 percent authentic. Thompson states that, "If your brand is positioned with someone in fake fatigues, it shows that you really don't care."

5. *Customize your messages and media buys to reach the subgroups within the military market* (e.g., gamers, golfers, spouses, families, Hispanics, Asians, African-Americans). Thompson states that, in working with clients that are marketing to the military, it is more beneficial to create your own custom network than to rely solely on traditional media buys. The more microscopic and targeted the message, the better.

FIGURE 18.1   Social media marketing targeted to military spouses

Here are a few examples of targeted, effective military marketing:

- A prepackaged produce supplier created special packaging for Kroger's supermarkets that included customized, prepaid calling cards with special military rates for calls from Iraq, Kuwait, and Afghanistan.

- Scion, the youth auto brand from Toyota, launched a car customization challenge strictly for active duty military personnel. The "Battle of the Builds" challenged service members to describe their vision of how they would customize a Scion xB with a $15,000 budget. Military personnel as well as civilians were able to vote for their favorite customized xB. Jack Hollis, vice president of Scion, stated, "Members of the military work as a team and have unmatched technical and mechanical skills. This contest is designed to let service members showcase these talents in a fun and exciting way. Creating a design competition especially for the military is one of the ways Scion thanks and salutes service men and women."

- The Apple iPhone has customized applications (apps) for military personnel. "Balancing work, family, and everything in between is a breeze, thanks to Apple's iPhone and apps. Customize your iPhone with these apps, and take your armed forces career to the next level," states the U.S. Army's home page. There are apps for Army first aid, the Army Study Guide (for soldiers preparing for a promotion), outdoor survival, and more. The copy on the web site

FIGURE 18.2   Military-Themed Cardstock

describes all the apps designed for military life and closes with, "With information like this, convince your commander that the iPhone is a necessary part of your field equipment . . . just remember to call home."

- Kmart carries military-themed card stock, in four varieties (Army, Navy, Marines, and Air Force). The card stock is marketed as "the perfect papers to add to scrapbook layouts featuring your favorite soldier!" And "all the card stock you need to celebrate the person you love in the Marines" (see Figure 18.2).

The military market may help expand your business. If your products or services are sold near a military base or you can create a product that would meet the needs of military personnel or their families, don't overlook this customer segment.

CHAPTER NINETEEN ▶▶
Vegetarians versus Meat Eaters

A friend of mine is a chiropractor who, last year, was trying to figure out how to grow his practice with new patients. He had marketed himself through the obvious channels: he'd partnered with massage therapists who would refer clients to him; he'd formed alliances with physicians and physical therapists, and he'd advertised in local gyms to reach people with sports injuries or muscle strain.

But he also wanted to reach a group of higher-income, educated people who are health conscious and also very interested in natural remedies. It made sense to target individuals who shared his values and beliefs of natural healing and how the body can heal itself when it is in proper alignment. He and I spoke at length about this and came to the conclusion that there may be a strong market for him in targeting individuals who are vegans and vegetarians.

Why? Because vegetarians are not just people with principles tied solely to the food they consume. Being vegetarian is about values, and not just values about which foods to eat. Most vegetarians are also greatly interested in health, animal welfare, and the environment. These values and areas of interest are highly compatible. It makes sense that someone who chooses not to eat meat would also care deeply about animal rights. Or if someone believes that consuming only plant-based foods is a healthier way to live, that person is also likely to be receptive to marketing messages that embrace natural and healthy lifestyle choices.

This is the beauty of values-based marketing: you can expand your business and sales by finding and targeting those people who share compatible values with what you're offering. You might not necessarily have thought about vegetarians as a "target customer" for a chiropractor. After all, most of us would think of targeting vegetarians with food- or beverage-related products. But if the core values of vegetarians and the principles of chiropractic medicine are *compatible,* there is tremendous potential in tapping into the relevant beliefs of vegetarians as a new customer group.

A San Francisco Bay Area real estate broker targeted his message to vegetarians. What do a real estate agent's eating habits have to do with his ability to sell houses? It's all about values.

Daniel Berman of Pacific Century Realty states on his web site (www.veggiereeltor.com) in an Open Letter to My Fellow Vegetarians:

> Why would it matter that you, as a vegetarian, have a real estate agent who is also a vegetarian? Simply stated, it's a matter of shared values, an approach to life and a way of relating to others. If you've been a vegetarian (or vegan) for any length of time, you know what I mean. I believe there is a need for people with my perspective, values and sensibilities, for a number of reasons, not the least of which is to offer an alternative.

The vegetarian market is enormous and very attractive to marketers because vegetarians tend to be educated, have higher-than-average incomes, and are willing to pay more for the products and services that fit their lifestyle. To reach vegetarians effectively, you first need to understand that there are several different levels of vegetarianism:

- *Vegans* eat no animal products at all, including eggs, dairy, or even honey.
- *Lacto-ovo vegetarians* eat no meat (including fish and poultry), but they do eat eggs and dairy.
- *Pescatarians* who are not really vegetarians, eat no meat except for fish.
- *Flexitarians,* who are also not vegetarians, but are concerned with eating healthy, have several meatless meals per week.

Here are some other facts worth noting: Compared to the total population, vegetarians are more likely to be female (62 percent of vegetarians are women, according to ConsumerStyles, a survey about consumer attitudes and behaviors) and the average age is 47. They're more highly educated than the general population. And they are passionate and plugged in: they stay on top of news and new products and eagerly share their thoughts, opinions, and endorsements about products they like or dislike. In fact, Adam Kochanowicz, senior editor of VegPage.com, states, "Vegans and vegetarians are some of the most loyal customers on the planet. As soon as one product hits the market specifically labeled as vegan-friendly, vegetarians hit the online forums to tell everyone. Their friends rush out to try it out, and assuming you have a decent product, you've developed product loyalty with an interest group tired of constantly having to research everyday products just so they can know it's safe to buy."

"Safe to buy" doesn't simply mean a food that doesn't contain animal products. For vegetarians and vegans, "safe to buy" can also mean products that were not tested on animals or products that are safe for the environment. Open the pantry and cabinets of vegetarians and you're likely to find shelves filled with green cleaning products, herbal shampoos and lotions, organic foods, and vitamins and supplements. Most of these types of products cost more, but vegetarians happily pay more for them because these products reflect their values and principles. "I'm not going to compromise my values to save a little money," says one friend of mine, who has been vegetarian for more than two decades.

Because vegetarians are also interested in health, the environment, and animal welfare, they're likely to go on eco-friendly vacations and donate to animal welfare and environmental causes. If you have a product or service that is compatible with these values and principles, marketing to vegetarians could be highly lucrative.

But beware: your product and company has to be authentically "vegetarian-friendly." Remember the importance of "operational readiness" that was discussed in Chapter 4? It applies here, too: if you're going to market yourself to vegans and vegetarians, your company and your products better be able to stand up to scrutiny. Consider this: a restaurant markets itself as serving organic, vegetarian food, but has seats that are made of leather. Imagine what a "disconnect" that would be! Or a top-of-the line, all-natural moisturizer was found to have been tested on animals. Or a cleaning solution is packaged in plastic that can't be easily recycled.

A few years ago, Mars UK, the British candy giant, introduced non-vegetarian whey to Mars and Snickers bars and immediately provoked major criticism from vegetarian groups. The company received more than 6,000 calls complaining about the change, and the company subsequently apologized to consumers and reversed its decision. Vegan and vegetarian consumers are very sensitive and very aware. Your company can't reach out to this group and expect to win their hearts and wallets if you don't sincerely embrace the philosophies and principles that drive their purchases.

REACHING VEGETARIANS

This educated, tech-savvy niche group is hungry for new products and information, so online marketing efforts are a great place to start. There is a tremendous amount of "chatter" online on this subject matter. Join the conversation through online ads, social media, and blogs. Direct mail can also be effective, but again, be aware of scrutiny: you'll want to let your recipients know that the mailer was created using recycled paper and soy-based ink, and is environmentally friendly. Local publications that target vegetarians or holistic living are avenues to explore. Often, these publications have a small but devoted and loyal readership. If you have such a publication in your area, offer to write an article as a guest contributor.

Do

- Use key terms like *fair trade, vegan, vegan-certified, not tested on animals,* and *organic.*
- Stress health benefits.
- Stress compassion for animals and the environment. Even a coffee cup can be marketed as "reusable" and therefore, better for the environment.
- Be authentic. It's better to be genuine and unpolished than "slick" and insincere. Your ads don't have to be beautiful. Just tell the truth and stress the core principles that vegetarians are interested in.
- Say it loud and say it proud. If your product is right for vegetarians, state that clearly. Take Bourgeois Boheme, for example. This is an international vegan fashion web site (www.bboheme.com) featuring shoes, belts, wallets, and apparel for men and women, with nothing made from animal products. Their tagline is "Fashion with Compassion," and the web site's home page states, "We believe that one should not trade ethics for fashion, nor sacrifice style for conscience." If your products are not tested on animals or contain no animal ingredients, let people know! State that clearly on the package.
- Check out the Vegetarian Society (www.vegsoc.org). This group offers great statistics that are helpful for business planning and even has a section on their web site called "Running a Business with Vegetarian Customers?" It gives great tips on reaching vegetarians and offers the official "Vegetarian Society approval" for products, services, and establishments. You can also advertise to their members and see how other businesses promote their products.
- Get involved! Sponsor a local event or become involved in National Vegetarian Week.
- Respond to all queries as promptly as possible. One blogger wrote about e-mailing Molton Brown, a British personal care company. The blogger wanted to know if Molton Brown products were tested on animals. He reported that within 15 minutes of sending his e-mail question, he had a reply from the company stating that it "never, ever tests products on animals." The blogger was just as pleased with the speed of the response as he was with the answer itself.

Don't

- Don't use vague words like *healthy,* which can mean anything or nothing.
- Don't misrepresent or skirt the truth. If your product package is made from 30 percent recycled ingredients, it's better to say that than to say "made from recycled materials," which implies that 100 percent of the package was made using recycled materials.

REACHING MEAT EATERS

Just as passionate about eating meat as vegans and vegetarians are about not eating it, meat eaters can be a viable customer segment, too. The segment may not attract as much attention as vegetarians, but that doesn't mean you should overlook it. For most meat eaters, it's not so much an "ideology" as it is something that is simply enjoyed. Nevertheless, there are groups and sites dedicated to the love of meat, and for some businesses and products, marketing to meat eaters makes good sense.

FIGURE 19.1   Meat Loving Buttons

Take the MeatEaters Ball, for example. An annual event, this gala held in California each year attracts hundreds of people who dress to the nines and eat, drink, and network. It's a "power" gala, attended by lots of successful, highly visible business executives. So it makes sense that Ferrari Beverly Hills is a sponsor. You certainly don't have to be a meat eater to own a Ferrari, but having a Ferrari sends a message. It says, "I'm rich, I'm flashy, and I'm living large." It's compatible with an event that would celebrate meat, since most steakhouses and top-of-the-line meat cuts are expensive. Furthermore, many business deals are made over an expensive meal featuring meat. So the "movers and shakers and dealmakers" who would likely attend the MeatEaters Ball are probably pretty good prospects for Ferrari Beverly Hills.

FIGURE 19.2   For Serious Bacon Lovers

What other types of business or products might find success with targeting meat eaters? Well, the first that come to mind are anything that has to do directly with cooking meat. Grills, cooking utensils, and related products are all a natural fit for targeting meat eaters. So are sporting events and sports enthusiasts. For many people, sporting events mean "tailgating parties" or having home parties where barbeque and burgers are served to hungry fans.

Hunting and fishing industries are also compatible. One web site, the Michigan Gun Owners (www.migunowners.org), declared March 20 as Michigan Meat Eaters Day and has a fan page on Facebook for people to show their support for "Michigan's hunting, fishing, agriculture, and meat-eating communities by signing on as a fan and posting photos and videos of you and your friends or family enjoying meat."

Meat eaters are a passionate group. There is a wide array of gimmicky products, such as T-shirts and buttons, even underwear, that show just how much people love meat (see Figures 19.1 and 19.2).

Conclusion

You're a smart business person. If you weren't, you wouldn't have picked up this book in the first place. You know that business is changing and that it's more important than ever to be relevant to your customers and keep evolving to meet their needs.

You also know that your community is changing. Your local community probably doesn't look anything like it did 10 years ago, and 10 years from now, it won't look anything like it does today. It's critical that you stay abreast of the changes in the market you serve and develop ways to tap into markets you're not currently serving, but should be. You are a smart, forward-thinking businessperson who is paying attention to the market shifts around you. This book has provided steps on how to identify new customer segments, narrowcast to reach them effectively, target them with relevant messages, and prepare your business operationally to ensure that you are "customer ready" and "customer friendly."

You are now ready to take what you've learned here and apply it to your business. You have the knowledge. You have the tools. Follow the steps and keep thinking, keep learning, keep paying attention to the shifts you see all around you—keep being the smart business person that you are. You can do it. You can market to people not like you. And when you do, you will see your sales, profits, and customer loyalty grow.

Index